Napoleon Hill's
Daily Inspiration
for
Everyday Women

by
Napoleon Hill
& Judith Williamson

A publication of
THE NAPOLEON HILL FOUNDATION

Published by:
The Napoleon Hill Foundation
P. O. Box 1277
Wise, Virginia USA 24293

Website: www.naphill.org
Email: napoleonhill@uvawise.edu

Napoleon Hill World Learning Center
Purdue University Calumet
2300 173rd Street
Hammond, Indiana 46323
Email: nhf@calumet.purdue.edu

Napoleon Hill's Daily Inspiration for Everyday Women
Editing by Judith A. Williamson
Formatting by Alan Chen
Cover by Uriel "Chino" Martinez

ISBN: 978-0-9819511-1-9

INTRODUCTION

Are you serious about success? If so, use this inspirational calendar to serve and remind you daily of your personal commitment to achieve your goals and lifelong purpose.

Designed for women, this inspirational tool enables you to focus on one or two of Dr. Hill's Success Principles per month. Brief descriptions of the 17 success principles align with the daily quotations.

Use this perpetual calendar to jumpstart your journey. As you set short-term and long-term goals for yourself, you will begin to see why many people turn to Dr. Hill for guidance and reassurance as they begin their personal quest toward success.

Good thoughts produce good outcomes. What you think about you become. Think on these quotations daily and set your sights on success. You will be surprised at how much you can achieve when you fine tune your focus and ready your aim.

Be your very best always.

Judy Williamson

Definiteness of Purpose

Definiteness of Purpose is the starting point of all achievement. All individual achievement begins with the adoption of a definite major purpose and a specific plan for its attainment. Without a purpose and a plan, people drift aimlessly throughout life. Lack of Definiteness of Purpose is the greatest stumbling block to 98 out of every 100 persons because they never really define their goals and start toward them with Definiteness of Purpose. Ideas form the foundation of all fortunes and the starting point of all inventions. Once a student learns how to harness the power of his mind and then how to organize the knowledge, he begins to keep his mind on the things he wants and off the things he does not want.

Obtaining a law degree and becoming a lawyer has inspired me to have persistence, personal initiative and concentrated effort.

—Christina Chia

January 1
Definiteness of Purpose

Everyone has inside him a piece of good news. The good news is that you don't yet realize how great you can be! How much you can love! What you can accomplish! And what your potential is!

— Anne Frank

The starting point of all personal achievement is the adoption of a Definite Major Purpose and a definite plan for its attainment.

— Napoleon Hill

Day 1

Definiteness of Purpose

A great goal in life is the only fortune worth finding.

— Jacqueline Kennedy Onassis

Definiteness of Purpose develops: self-reliance, personal initiative, imagination, enthusiasm, self-discipline, and concentration of effort.

— Napoleon Hill

Day 2

January 3
Definiteness of Purpose

Let me listen to me and not to them.
                                    — Gertrude Stein

Definiteness of Purpose encourages you to specialize in success.
                                    — Napoleon Hill

Day 3

Definiteness of Purpose

Don't let people tell you who you are.

— Diane Sawyer

Definiteness of Purpose encourages budgeting of time and money so efforts remain focused on attaining your Definite Major Purpose.

— Napoleon Hill

Day 4

January 5

Definiteness of Purpose

All of us can take steps—no matter how small and insignificant at the start—in the direction we want to go.

— Marsha Sinetar

Definiteness of Purpose alerts the mind to opportunities and gives courage for action.

— Napoleon Hill

Day 5

Definiteness of Purpose

If you don't have a dream, how can you have a dream come true?

— Faye LaPointe

Definiteness of Purpose helps develop the capacity to reach decisions.

— Napoleon Hill

Day 6

January 7

Definiteness of Purpose

A year from now you may wish you had started today.

— Karen Lamb

Definiteness of Purpose inspires the cooperation of others.

— Napoleon Hill

Day 7

Definiteness of Purpose

Unfulfilled desires are the dangerous forces.

— Sarah Tarleton Colvin

Definiteness of Purpose prepares the mind for faith.

— Napoleon Hill

Day 8

January 9

Definiteness of Purpose

I am not afraid . . . I was born to do this.

— Joan of Arc

Definiteness of Purpose provides a success consciousness.

— Napoleon Hill

Day 9

Definiteness of Purpose

We conceive children and we conceive projects.

— Julia Cameron

All individual achievements are the result of a motive or a combination of motives. There are nine basic motives inspiring all voluntary action.

— Napoleon Hill

Day 10

January 11

Definiteness of Purpose

*Maturity is achieved when you
understand that one has to decide.*

— *Angela B. McBride*

Motive One:
*—the emotion of love (greatest of all
motives).*

— *Napoleon Hill*

Day 11

Definiteness of Purpose

*Never confuse knowledge with wisdom.
One helps you earn a living, the other
helps you build a life.*

— Sandra Carey

*Motive Two:
—the emotion of sex.*

— Napoleon Hill

Day 12

January 13

Definiteness of Purpose

*The most important thing is not what
destiny does to us, but what we do with it.*
                                    — Florence Nightingale

Motive Three:
—the desire for material gain.
                                    — Napoleon Hill

Day 13

Definiteness of Purpose

I want to do it because I want to do it.
Women must try to do things as men have
tried. When they fail, their failure must
be but a challenge to others.

— Amelia Earhart

Motive Four:
—the desire for self-preservation.

— Napoleon Hill

Day 14

January 15
Definiteness of Purpose

This is happiness; to be dissolved into something complete and great.

— *Willa Cather*

Motive Five:
—the desire for freedom of body and mind.

— *Napoleon Hill*

Day 15

Definiteness of Purpose

How wrong it is for woman to expect the man to build the world she wants, rather than to set out to create it for herself.

— Anaïs Nin

Motive Six:
—the desire for self-expression and recognition.

— Napoleon Hill

Day 16

January 17
Definiteness of Purpose

Figuring out who you are is the whole point of the human experience.

— *Anna Quindlen*

Motive Seven:
—the desire for life after death.

— *Napoleon Hill*

Day 17

Definiteness of Purpose

Action is the antidote to despair.

— Joan Baez

Motive Eight:
—the desire for revenge.

— Napoleon Hill

Day 18

January 19

Definiteness of Purpose

My will shall shape my future. Whether I fail or succeed shall be no man's doing but my own. I am the force; I can clear any obstacle before me or I can be lost in the maze. My choice; my responsibility; win or lose, only I hold the key to my destiny.
— Elaine Maxwell

Motive Nine:
—the emotion of fear.

— Napoleon Hill

Day 19

Definiteness of Purpose

It is only the first step that is difficult.

— Marie De Vichy-Chaconne

Any dominating idea, plan or purpose held in the mind through repetition of thought and emotionalized with a burning desire for its realization, is taken over by the subconscious mind and acted upon through whatever natural and logical means may be available.

— Napoleon Hill

Day 20

January 21

Definiteness of Purpose

*If you doubt you can accomplish
something, then you can't accomplish it.
You have to have confidence in your
ability, and then be tough enough to
follow through.*

— *Rosalynn Carter*

Conscious Mind

- *reasoning/thinking*
  faculty
- *deliberates, analyzes*
- *selects Definite*
  Major Purpose
- *guardian of*
  subconscious

Subconscious Mind

- *natural,*
  uncultivated mind
  responds
  instinctively to
  emotion
- *develops the power*
  of will

— *Napoleon Hill*

Day 21

Definiteness of Purpose

*One ship drives east and another drives
west*
With the selfsame winds that blow.
'Tis the set of the sails
And not the gales
Which tells us the way to go.
— Ella Wheeler Wilcox

*Any dominating desire, plan or purpose
which is backed by faith is taken over by
the subconscious mind.*
— Napoleon Hill

Day 22

January 23
Definiteness of Purpose

Many persons have a wrong idea about what constitutes true happiness. It is not attained through self-gratification, but through fidelity to a worthy purpose.

— *Helen Keller*

Creative genius lies within the power of the subconscious mind.

— *Napoleon Hill*

Day 23

Definiteness of Purpose

*One could always point to a time, a choice,
an act that set the tone for a life and
changed a personal destiny.*

— *Carol O'Connell*

*The nine factors responsible for
developing creative genius are:
Definiteness of Purpose, Applied Faith,
Enthusiasm, Imagination, Motive,
Personal Initiative, Habit of Going the
Extra Mile, Master Mind Alliance, and
Positive Mental Attitude.*

— *Napoleon Hill*

Day 24

January 25

Definiteness of Purpose

*Since we are capable of change and
modifications, the future will be in many
ways only as good as we have the courage
to make it.*

— June Tapp

*The power of thought is the only thing
over which any human being has
complete, unquestionable control.*

— Napoleon Hill

Day 25

Definiteness of Purpose

You were born God's original. Try not to become someone's copy.

— Marian Wright Edelman

The subconscious mind appears to be the only doorway of individual approach to Infinite Intelligence, and it is capable of being influenced by the individual.

— Napoleon Hill

Day 26

January 27

Definiteness of Purpose

For what is done or learned by one class of women becomes, by virtue of their common womanhood, the property of all women.
— Elizabeth Blackwell

Every brain is both a broadcasting station and a receiving set for the vibrations of thought – a fact which explains the importance of moving with Definiteness of Purpose instead of drifting along in life – since the brain may be so charged with definiteness of purpose that it will begin to attract the physical appearance of that purpose.
— Napoleon Hill

Day 27

Definiteness of Purpose

The thing women have got to learn is that nobody gives you power. You just take it.

— Roseanne Barr

Nothing can be achieved unless one is willing to give something in return.

— Napoleon Hill

Day 28

January 29
Definiteness of Purpose

All my life I've wanted to be somebody, but I see now I should have been more specific.

— Jane Wagner

Write out a clear, concise plan by which you intend to achieve your definite major purpose. Keep this plan to yourself, except for members of your Mastermind Alliance.

— Napoleon Hill

Day 29

Definiteness of Purpose

Failing to plan is planning to fail.

— Effie Jones

*Keep your mind on the things you want
and off the things you do not want.*

— Napoleon Hill

Day 30

January 31
Definiteness of Purpose

We are weaving the future on the loom of today.

— Grace Dawson

Remember: Your only limitation is that which you set up in your own mind by your neglect in keeping your mental attitude positive.

— Napoleon Hill

Day 31

Master Mind Alliance

The Mastermind Alliance principle consists of an alliance of two or more minds working together in perfect harmony for the attainment of a definite objective. Success does not come without the cooperation of others. The Mastermind Alliance principle is a practical medium through which you may appropriate and use the full benefits of the experience, training, education, specialized knowledge, and native intelligence of others as completely as if it were your own. An active alliance of two or more minds, in a spirit of perfect harmony for the attainment of a common objective, stimulates each mind to a higher degree of courage than that ordinarily experienced, and paves the way for the state of mind known as Faith.

In collegiate Women's Basketball, each team is an organized Master Mind unit unique to itself. It is a requirement of each player to know intuitively what the other players are thinking. In this manner, you maintain the winning edge.

— Kelley Watts

February 1
Master Mind Alliance

If you don't look out for others, who will look out for you?

— *Whoopi Goldberg*

The Master Mind principle consists of an alliance of two or more minds working in perfect harmony for the attainment of a definite objective.

— *Napoleon Hill*

Day 32

Master Mind Alliance

*If you have knowledge, let others light
their candles at it.*

— *Margaret Fuller*

*The Master Mind principle is a practical
medium through which you may
appropriate and use the full benefits of the
experience, the training, the education,
the specialized knowledge and native
intelligence of other people, as completely
as if they were your own.*

— *Napoleon Hill*

Day 33

February 3
Master Mind Alliance

*Never doubt that a small group of
thoughtful, committed people can change
the world; indeed it is the only thing
that ever has.*

—Margaret Mead

*An active alliance of two or more minds in
a spirit of perfect harmony for the
attainment of a common objective,
stimulates each mind to a higher degree of
courage than that ordinarily experienced,
and paves the way for that state of mind
known as faith.*

— Napoleon Hill

Day 34

Master Mind Alliance

What is unity, so it is understood, is two diverse things made one.

— *Saint Theresa*

Once a Master Mind Alliance is formed, the group as a whole must become and remain active.

— *Napoleon Hill*

Day 35

February 5
Master Mind Alliance

The ones that give, get back in kind.
— Pam Durban

The group must move on a definite plan,
at a definite time, toward a definite
common objective.

— Napoleon Hill

Day 36

Master Mind Alliance

Women now know that, besides hard work and lots of skill, the move to the top requires a supportive network.

— June E. Gabler

There must be a complete meeting of the minds. Discord is not permitted.

— Napoleon Hill

Day 37

February 7
Master Mind Alliance

A burning purpose attracts others who are drawn along with it and help fulfill it.
> *— Margaret Bourke-White*

A Master Mind Alliance, properly conducted, stimulates each mind in the alliance to move with enthusiasm, personal initiative, and imagination and accelerates the capacity of the minds in the alliance to receive and transmit thought vibrations through telepathy and the sixth sense.
> *— Napoleon Hill*

Day 38

Master Mind Alliance

We should acknowledge differences, we should greet differences, until difference makes no difference anymore.

— *Dr. Adela A. Allen*

The Master Mind principle, when actively applied, has the effect of connecting the subconscious sections of the minds of the allies, and gives each member full access to the spiritual powers of all the other members.

— *Napoleon Hill*

Day 39

February 9
Master Mind Alliance

*The greatest gift of human beings is that
we have the power of empathy.*

— Meryl Streep

*It is a matter of established record that all
individual successes, based upon any kind
of achievement above mediocrity, are
attained through the Master Mind
principle.*

— Napoleon Hill

Day 40

Master Mind Alliance

*When we speak of informal leadership, we
describe . . . the capacity of the
organization to create the leadership that
best suits its needs at the time.*

— Meg Wheatley

*One type of Master Mind is for purely
social or personal reasons, consisting of
one's relatives, friends and religious
advisers, where no material gain is
sought.*

— Napoleon Hill

Day 41

February 11
Master Mind Alliance

*Never one thing and seldom one person
can make for a success. It takes a number
of them merging into one perfect whole.*
— *Marie Dressler*

*The other type of Master Mind is the
occupational, business or professional
alliance, consisting of individuals who
have a motive of a material or financial
nature; in other words, an economic
alliance, designed to help you sell your
personal services, your skill, your ability,
or to help you succeed in business.*
— *Napoleon Hill*

Day 42

Master Mind Alliance

Our ability to connect our energy, our hearts, our presence, our intuition, and our healing to other beings is perhaps our greatest resource. Once we master the element of contact, we can heal others as we are being healed.

— Laura Day

There are Twelve Great Riches that individuals aspire to in life. They are: a positive mental attitude, sound physical health, harmony in human relationships, freedom from fear, the hope of achievement, the capacity for faith, willingness to share one's blessings, a labor of love, an open mind on all subjects, self-discipline, the capacity to understand people, and financial security.
— Napoleon Hill

Day 43

February 13
Master Mind Alliance

Speak to yourself as if what you desire is already true and it already is.

— Ruth Ross Ressler

Step 1: *Adopt a Definite Purpose as an objective to be attained by the alliance choosing individual members whose education, experience, and influence are such as to make them of the greatest value in achieving that purpose.*

— Napoleon Hill

Day 44

Master Mind Alliance

*Don't go to your grave without flying a
kite, skipping rope, going barefoot,
catching fireflies, and jumping
in a mud puddle. Let go and live.*

— Barbara Jenkins

Step 2: *Determine what appropriate
benefit each member may receive in return
for her cooperation in the alliance.*

— Napoleon Hill

Day 45

February 15
Master Mind Alliance

*A soul occupied with great ideas best
performs small duties.*

— Harriet Martineau

Step 3: *Establish a definite place where
the members of the alliance will meet,
have a definite plan, and arrange a
definite time for the mutual discussion of
the plan.*

— Napoleon Hill

Day 46

Master Mind Alliance

To do good things in the world, first you must know who you are and what gives meaning to your life.

— *Paula P. Brownlee*

Step 4: *It is the burden of the leader of the alliance to see that harmony among all the members is maintained and that action is continuous in the pursuance of the Definite Major Objective.*

— *Napoleon Hill*

Day 47

February 17
Master Mind Alliance

It is difficult to see things clearly if the shadow of doubt diminishes the light entering your eyes.

— Sophia Bedford-Pierce

Step 5: *The watchword of the alliance should be Definiteness of Purpose, Positiveness of Plan, backed by continuous perfect harmony.*

— Napoleon Hill

Day 48

Master Mind Alliance

Goals are a joint effort process: getting in touch with our heart and setting a course; then depending on and being willing for God to direct us one step at a time.

— Sheila West

Step 6: *The number of individuals in an alliance should be governed entirely by the nature and magnitude of the purpose to be attained.*

— Napoleon Hill

Day 49

February 19
Master Mind Alliance

After all is said and done, relationships are truly the only things that really matter.

— Lee Ezell

Begin at once to establish a true Master Mind Alliance. Select individuals you accept and who accept you. Do not choose someone just because you like her.

— Napoleon Hill

Day 50

Master Mind Alliance

My mission is to travel globally extracting diamonds out of people's dust.

— Thelma L. Wells

When the members of your alliance have been selected, take them into your absolute confidence regarding your purposes and plans.

— Napoleon Hill

Day 51

February 21
Master Mind Alliance

Leave old or new ideas where they prove harmful. Leave the bad for the good. Leave good things for better things.
— Barbara Roberts Pine

Don't tell any one else of the alliance. Reveal your desires and plans only to the members of your Master Mind Alliance.
— Napoleon Hill

Day 52

Master Mind Alliance

Freedom is not the right to do what we want but the power to do what we ought.

— Corrie Ten Boom

Work out a schedule for contacting each other frequently.

— Napoleon Hill

Day 53

Master Mind Alliance

In great moments life seems neither right nor wrong, but something greater, it seems inevitable.

— Margaret Sherwood

At each meeting have a report of your individual and collective progress toward the goal.

— Napoleon Hill

Day 54

Master Mind Alliance

*You don't manage people; you manage
things. You lead people.*

> — *Admiral Grace Hopper*

*At the first sign of any lack of harmony
among the members, find out what is
causing it.*

> — *Napoleon Hill*

Day 55

February 25
Master Mind Alliance

Without the burden of afflictions it is impossible to reach the height of grace. The gifts of grace increase as the struggles increase.

— Saint Rose of Lima

If the negative attitude of any particular member is causing the lack of harmony, deal with the problem at once.

— Napoleon Hill

Day 56

Master Mind Alliance

*The biggest handicap in the world is
negative thinking.*

> — Heather Whitestone

*If required, remove the negative member
from the group. Otherwise, convert the
member to the principles of this
philosophy.*

> — Napoleon Hill

Day 57

February 27
Master Mind Alliance

Each person grows not only by her own talents or development of her inner beliefs, but also by what she receives from the persons around her.

— *Iris Haberli*

Keep your mind positive and receptive at all times. Especially when you appear before your Master Mind group.

— *Napoleon Hill*

Day 58

Master Mind Alliance

Whenever people think of success, they immediately think of "more"—more love, more fun and good times, more respect. Yet, upon examination, success is not about having more. It is about fine-tuning your understanding of what you are willing to give up in order to get what you really want.

— Chin-Ning Chu

Get on good terms with yourself as you work to develop a successful Master Mind Alliance with others.

— Napoleon Hill

Day 59

Applied Faith

Faith is an active state of mind. This belief in yourself is applied to achieving a definite major purpose in life. Faith is an abstract idea, a purely mental concept. Faith is the activity of individual minds facing themselves and establishing a working association with Infinite Intelligence. When a plan comes through to your conscious mind while you are open to the guidance of Infinite Intelligence, accept it with appreciation and gratitude and act on it at once. Do not hesitate, do not argue, challenge, worry, fret about it, or wonder if it's right. Act on it! Action is the first requirement of all faith. As the Bible states: "Faith without works is dead."

Applied Faith generates appropriate resourcefulness from within and augments mastery and competence.

—*Therese G. Sullivan*

March 1

Applied Faith

I took an inventory and looked into my little bag to see what I had left over. I had one jewel left in the bag, the brightest jewel of all. I had the gift of faith.

— *Lola Falana*

Faith is a state of mind which you may develop by conditioning your mind to receive Infinite Intelligence.

— *Napoleon Hill*

Day 60

Applied Faith

Nothing contributes so much to tranquilizing the mind as a steady purpose – a point on which the soul may fix its intellectual eye.

— *Mary Wollstonecraft Shelley*

Applied faith is adapting the power received from Infinite Intelligence to a Definite Major Purpose.

— *Napoleon Hill*

Day 61

March 3

Applied Faith

Throughout the centuries there were men who took first steps down new roads armed with nothing but their own vision.
— Ayn Rand

Faith is the state of mind in which you contact the power of Infinite Intelligence and focus it upon the object of your desire.
— Napoleon Hill

Day 62

Applied Faith

Sorrow looks back. Worry looks round.
Faith looks ahead.

— Beatrice Fallon

Faith is a state of mind wherein you
temporarily relax your reason and will
power, and open your mind completely to
the guidance of Infinite Intelligence for
the attainment of some definite purpose.

— Napoleon Hill

Day 63

March 5

Applied Faith

Not truth, but faith, it is, that keeps the world alive.

— Edna St. Vincent Millay

The guidance comes in the form of an idea or plan which comes to you while you are in this receptive attitude.

— Napoleon Hill

Day 64

Applied Faith

*But in this season it is well to reassert
that the hope of mankind rests in faith.
As man thinketh, so he is. Nothing much
happens unless you believe in it, and
believing there is hope for the world is a
way to move toward it.*

— Gladys Taber

*The subconscious mind is the gateway
between our conscious mind and the vast
reservoir of Infinite Intelligence.*

— Napoleon Hill

Day 65

Applied Faith

There is nothing to fear except the persistent refusal to find out the truth, the persistent refusal to analyze the causes of happenings. Fear grows in darkness; if you think there's a bogeyman around, turn on the light.

— *Dorothy Thompson*

The power of Infinite Intelligence pours life into us as a flowing stream, maintaining all of the functions of our bodies and minds, and we can use it to guide and govern the circumstances and conditions of our lives, if we will act as conductors of this energy and shape it according to our constructive purposes.

— *Napoleon Hill*

Day 66

Applied Faith

To have faith where you cannot see; to be willing to work on in the dark; to be conscious of the fact that, so long as you strive for the best, there are better things on the way, this in itself is success.

— Katherine Logan

If you would have faith – keep your mind on that which you want and off that which you do not want.

— Napoleon Hill

Day 67

March 9

Applied Faith

*. . . There are more awakenings than
births in a life.*

— Dorothy Thompson

Steps to Faith:
- *Express a definite desire for the
  achievement of a purpose and relate it
  to one or more of the basic motives.*
- *Create a definite and specific plan for
  the attainment of that desire.*
- *Start acting on that plan, putting every
  conscious effort behind it.*

  — Napoleon Hill

Day 68

Applied Faith

The things that matter the most in this world, they can never be held in our hand.

— Gloria Gaither

When the plan comes through to your conscious mind, accept it with appreciation and gratitude and act on it at once!

— Napoleon Hill

Day 69

March 11

Applied Faith

*Aspire to be, and all that we are not God
will give us credit for trying.*

> — *Nannie Burroughs*

*Accept with gratitude a plan by means of
which you can fulfill your desires through
the rule of hard work backed by a burning
desire.*

> — *Napoleon Hill*

Day 70

Applied Faith

Aspiration is the seed of life.

— Joan Chittister

You must give an equivalent value for the object of your desires!

— Napoleon Hill

Day 71

March 13

Applied Faith

After all it is those who have a deep and real inner life who are best able to deal with the irritating details of outer life.

— Evelyn Underhill

When you pray, make your prayer an expression of gratitude and thanksgiving for the blessings you have already received.

— Napoleon Hill

Day 72

Applied Faith

The passage is through, not over, not by, not around, but through.

— *Cherrie Moraga*

To succeed in life you must rid yourself of the negative influences of fear before faith can come into your mind.

— *Napoleon Hill*

Day 73

March 15

Applied Faith

*Sometimes when you think you are done,
it is just the edge of beginning. Probably
that's why we decide we're done. It's
getting scary. We are touching down onto
something real. It is beyond the point
when you think you are done that often
something strong comes out.*
                    — Natalie Goldberg

*Fear of poverty is the most destructive of
fears and also the most difficult to master.*
                    — Napoleon Hill

Day 74

Applied Faith

We know God wipes away all tears, but it certainly feels good when He uses human hands.

> — *Mary Paulson-Lauda*

Fear of criticism is almost as general as the fear of poverty.

> — *Napoleon Hill*

Day 75

March 17

Applied Faith

When you come to the edge of all the light you know, and are about to step off into the darkness of the unknown, faith is knowing one of two things will happen: there will be something solid to stand on, or you will be taught how to fly.
> — *Barbara J. Winter*

Fear of ill health is related to the fear of death. There is overwhelming evidence that a disease can originate as a negative thought which the person continues to sell to herself until through auto-suggestion physical symptoms actually appear.
> — *Napoleon Hill*

Day 76

Applied Faith

*Put even the plainest woman into a
beautiful dress and unconsciously she will
try to live up to it.*

— Lady Duff-Gordon

*Most doctors now agree that there is a
definite relationship between the patient's
mental attitude and her physical
condition.*

— Napoleon Hill

Day 77

March 19

Applied Faith

I think wholeness comes from living your life consciously during the day and then exploring your inner life or unconscious at night.

— *Margery Cuyler*

You can guarantee yourself sound physical health by maintaining a positive mental attitude and developing a sound health consciousness whereby you expect, demand and receive health-sustaining elements from your food, the fresh air and sunshine!

— *Napoleon Hill*

Day 78

Applied Faith

Don't spend time beating on a wall,
hoping to transform it into a door.

— Dr. Laura Schlessinger

Fear of the loss of love is the basis of
jealousy and overly-dependent
relationships.

— Napoleon Hill

Day 79

Applied Faith

I never feel age . . . . If you have creative work, you don't have age or time.

— Louise Nevelson

Fear of old age is related to a person's need to be needed.

— Napoleon Hill

Day 80

Applied Faith

*I make the most of all that comes, and the
least of all that goes.*

— *Sara Teasdale*

*Fear of loss of liberty is related to a
person's need to feel independent and
autonomous.*

— *Napoleon Hill*

Day 81

March 23

Applied Faith

Begin doing what you want to do now. We are not living in eternity. We have only this moment, sparkling like a star in our hand – and melting like a snowflake. Let us use it before it is too late.

— Marie Beyon Ray

Fear of death is a universal fear and seems related to a person's need to feel a sense of worth validated by continued life.

— Napoleon Hill

Day 82

Applied Faith

You can have anything you want if you want it desperately enough. You must want it with an inner exuberance that erupts through the skin and joins the energy that created the world.

— *Sheila Graham*

The mind attracts to it the counterpart of that which it dwells upon.

— *Napoleon Hill*

Day 83

Applied Faith

*I invented my life by taking for granted
that everything I did not like would have
an opposite which I would like.*

— *Coco Chanel*

*Before the state of mind known as faith
will produce practical results, it must be
expressed in some form of action.*

— *Napoleon Hill*

Day 84

Applied Faith

For you to be successful, sacrifices must be made. It's better that they are made by others but failing that, you'll have to make them yourself.

— Rita Mae Brown

Faith is the act of believing by doing.
— Napoleon Hill

Day 85

March 27

Applied Faith

People always call it luck when you've acted more sensibly than they have.

— Anne Tyler

One of the greatest things you can do with applied faith is to refuse to think about things you do not want and feed your mind on the things you do want until you start getting them.

— Napoleon Hill

Day 86

Applied Faith

At the worst, a house unkept cannot be so distressing as a life unlived.

— *Dame Rose Macaulay*

Faith without works is dead.

— *Napoleon Hill*

Day 87

Applied Faith

*Life is about not knowing, having to
change, taking the moment and making
the best of it, without knowing what's
going to happen next. Delicious
ambiguity.*

— *Gilda Radner*

*Faith can give you the strength to move
through temporary defeat.*

— *Napoleon Hill*

Day 88

Applied Faith

With faith as my crutch I've found peace,
one of the few things I have left which is
strictly my own.

— Nancy Reagan

Faith can tune you into the possibilities
existing even within defeat.

— Napoleon Hill

Day 89

March 31

Applied Faith

When you can't have what you want, it's time to start wanting what you have.

— Kathleen A. Sutton

Faith can help you discover that every adversity carries with it the seed of an equivalent or greater benefit.

— Napoleon Hill

Day 90

Going the Extra Mile

Going the Extra Mile is the action of rendering more and better service than that for which you are presently paid. When you Go The Extra Mile, the Law of Compensation comes into play. This Universal Law neither permits any living thing to get something for nothing nor allows any form of labor to go unrewarded. You will find that Mother Nature goes the extra mile in everything that she does. She doesn't create just barely enough of each gene or species to get by; she produces an over abundance to take care of all emergencies that arise and still have enough left to guarantee the perpetuation of each form of life.

. . . taking the initiative came naturally to me. It wasn't until my adult years that I realized how far my initiative had taken me in life.
— *Maureen E. Muha*

April 1

Going the Extra Mile

Let no one come to you without leaving better.

— *Mother Teresa*

Going the Extra Mile places the Law of Increasing Returns at your command and working for your benefit.

— *Napoleon Hill*

Day 91

Going the Extra Mile

If we keep on doin' what we always done,
we'll keep on gettin' what we always got.

— *Barbara Lyon*

The habit of doing more than that for
which you are being paid causes you to
benefit by the Law of Compensation
through which no act or deed will or can
be expressed without an equivalent
reaction after its own kind.

— *Napoleon Hill*

Day 92

April 3

Going the Extra Mile

*If someone listens, or stretches out a hand,
or whispers a kind word of
encouragement, or attempts to understand
a lonely person, extraordinary things
begin to happen.*

— *Loretta Girzartis*

*You must render the greatest amount of
service of which you are capable and
render it in a friendly, positive manner.*

— *Napoleon Hill*

Day 93

Going the Extra Mile

Do not save your loving speeches
For your friends till they are dead;
Do not write them on their tombstones,
Speak them rather now instead.

— Anna Cummins

You must do this regardless of your
immediate compensation – even if it
appears that you will receive no
immediate compensation whatsoever!

— Napoleon Hill

Day 94

April 5

Going the Extra Mile

An effort made for the happiness of others lifts us above ourselves.

— Lydia M. Child

Until a man, begins to render more service than that for which he is paid, he is not entitled to more pay than he receives for that service, since, obviously, he is already receiving full pay for what he does!

— Napoleon Hill

Day 95

Going the Extra Mile

*Great opportunities to help others seldom
come, but small ones surround us every
day.*

— Sally Koch

*98 out of 100 wage earners have no
Definite Purpose greater than that of
working for a daily wage. Therefore, no
matter how much work they do, or how
well they do it, the "wheel of fortune" turns
past them without giving them more than
a bare living, because they neither expect
nor demand more!*

— Napoleon Hill

Day 96

April 7

Going the Extra Mile

Little deeds of kindness, little words of love,
Help to make earth happy like the heaven above.

— Julia A. Fletcher Carney

The habit of doing more than you are paid for will bring you to the favorable attention of those who have opportunities to offer.

— Napoleon Hill

Day 97

Going the Extra Mile

For life is the mirror of king and slave,
Tis just what we are and do;
Then give to the world the best you have,
And the best will come back to you.
                    — Madeleine Bridges

You will never command more than
average compensation until you become
indispensable to somebody or some group.
                    — Napoleon Hill

Day 98

April 9

Going the Extra Mile

No man is better than his service for the betterment of others.

— Candice M. Pope

Going the Extra Mile leads to your mental growth and physical perfection in various forms of service, thereby developing a greater ability and skill in your chosen vocation.

— Napoleon Hill

Day 99

Going the Extra Mile

*You have to recognize when the right place
and the right time fuse and take
advantage of that opportunity. There are
plenty of opportunities out there. You
can't sit back and wait.*

— *Ellen Metcalf*

*Going the Extra Mile protects you against
the loss of employment and places you in a
position to choose your own job and
working conditions.*

— *Napoleon Hill*

Day 100

April 11

Going the Extra Mile

*If you really want something, you can
figure out how to make it happen.*

— *Cher*

*Going the Extra Mile turns the spotlight
on you and gives you the benefit of the
Law of Contrast, which is very important
in advertising yourself.*

— *Napoleon Hill*

Day 101

Going the Extra Mile

Life is not easy for any of us. But what of that? We must have perseverance and above all confidence in ourselves. We must believe that we are gifted for something and that this thing, at whatever cost, must be attained.

— Madame Curie

Doing more than you are immediately paid for leads to the development of a positive, pleasing attitude, which is among the more important traits of a Pleasing Personality.

— Napoleon Hill

Day 102

April 13

Going the Extra Mile

When we deliberately leave the safety of
the shore of our lives, we surrender to a
mystery beyond our intent.

— Ann Linnea

Going the Extra Mile definitely gives you
greater confidence in yourself and puts
you on a better basis with your own
conscience.

— Napoleon Hill

Day 103

Going the Extra Mile

You can't build a reputation on what you intend to do.

— *Liz Smith*

Going the Extra Mile aids one in overcoming the destructive habit of procrastination.

— *Napoleon Hill*

Day 104

Going the Extra Mile

*Great thoughts speak only to the
thoughtful mind, but great actions speak
to all mankind.*

— Emily P. Bissell

*Going the Extra Mile helps you develop
Definiteness of Purpose, without which
one cannot hope for success.*

— Napoleon Hill

Day 105

Going the Extra Mile

This has always been a motto of mine: Attempt the impossible in order to improve your work.

— Bette Davis

If you never do anything more than you get paid for, you'll never get paid for anything more than you do.

— Napoleon Hill

Day 106

April 17

Going the Extra Mile

Life is change. Growth is optional.
Choose wisely.

— Karen Kaiser Clark

The habit of Going the Extra Mile is one
which you may adopt and follow on your
own initiative without asking the
permission of anyone to do so.

— Napoleon Hill

Day 107

Going the Extra Mile

Women share with men the need for personal success, even the taste for power, and no longer are we willing to satisfy those needs through the achievements of surrogates, whether husbands, children, or merely role models.

— Elizabeth Dole

Quality of service rendered + Quantity of service rendered + the Mental Attitude in which it is rendered = your compensation.

— Napoleon Hill

Day 108

Going the Extra Mile

*When we are magnanimous, liberal in
our giving as well as in sharing of our
self, we show noble character and an
abundance of spirit and strength.*

— Alexandra Stoddard

$$Q^1 + Q^2 + MA = Compensation$$
— Napoleon Hill

Day 109

Going the Extra Mile

*I refuse to believe that trading recipes is
silly. Tunafish casserole is at least as real
as corporate stock.*

— *Barbara Grizzuti Harrison*

*Each time you perform an act with the
attitude that you are going to excel all of
your previous achievements you are really
growing.*

— *Napoleon Hill*

Day 110

April 21

Going the Extra Mile

*Striving for excellence motivates you;
striving for perfection is demoralizing.*

— Harriet Braiker

*Going the Extra Mile is one way of writing
yourself an insurance policy against the
fear of poverty, fear of want, and against
the low pay competition of the "clock
watcher."*

— Napoleon Hill

Day 111

Going the Extra Mile

*One must think like a hero to behave like
a merely decent human being.*

— May Sarton

*Going the Extra Mile turns the spotlight
on you and gives you the benefit of the
Law of Contrast, a good way to advertise
yourself.*

— Napoleon Hill

Day 112

April 23

Going the Extra Mile

*From where you sit, you can probably
reach out with comparative ease and
touch a life of serenity and peace. You can
wait for things to happen and not get too
sad when they don't. That's fine for some
but not for me. Serenity is pleasant, but it
lacks the ecstasy of achievement.*

— *Estee Lauder*

*The habit of rendering more and better
service than you are immediately
compensated for develops the habit of
Personal Initiative.*

— *Napoleon Hill*

Day 113

Going the Extra Mile

Happiness is not a station to arrive at.
But a manner of traveling.

— Margaret Lee Runbeck

Personal Initiative means doing the thing
that needs to be done without somebody
telling you to do it.

— Napoleon Hill

Day 114

Going the Extra Mile

The only place you'll find success before work is in the dictionary.

> — *May B. Smith*

Don't wait for things to happen, make them happen.

> — *Napoleon Hill*

Day 115

Going the Extra Mile

The way I see it, if you want the rainbow, you've got to be willing to put up with the rain.

— Dolly Parton

You know, sometimes the hardest gal in the world to get along with is the one walking around under your own hat.

— Napoleon Hill

Day 116

Going the Extra Mile

The great thing to learn about life is, first, not to do what you don't want to do, and, second, to do what you do want to do.

— Margaret Anderson

It pays to be on good terms with your own conscious.

— Napoleon Hill

Day 117

Going the Extra Mile

The more we give of anything, the more we shall get back.

— *Grace Speare*

You must do what you are paid for, to keep the job, but you have the privilege of rendering an overplus of service as a means of accumulating a reserve credit of goodwill which entitles you to higher pay and a better position.

— *Napoleon Hill*

Day 118

April 29

Going the Extra Mile

As long as you keep a person down, some part of you has to be down there to hold him down, so it means you cannot soar as you otherwise might.

— Marian Anderson

If the type of service you are trained to render does not bring the compensation you feel that you require, then possibly you should consider a change of occupation.

— Napoleon Hill

Day 119

Going the Extra Mile

When it comes to getting things done, we need fewer architects and more bricklayers.

— Colleen C. Barrett

The habit of Going the Extra Mile is one which you may adopt and follow on your own initiative, without asking the permission of anyone to do so.

— Napoleon Hill

Day 120

Pleasing Personality

Personality is the sum total of one's mental, spiritual, and physical traits and habits that distinguish one from all others. It is the factor that determines whether one is liked or disliked by others. Your personality is your greatest asset or liability. It embraces everything you control—mind, body and soul. Some characteristics of a pleasing personality include: positive mental attitude, flexibility, sincerity, prompt actions, courtesy, tactfulness, pleasing tone of voice, smile, and tolerance.

In my experience having a pleasing personality is really about being conscious of those around you, really caring about what is important to them.

— Adora Spencer

May 1

Pleasing Personality

There's always room for improvement—
it's the biggest room in the house.

— Louise Heath Leber

Every person achieving a high degree of
personal success has mastered the art of
successfully selling herself.

— Napoleon Hill

Day 121

Pleasing Personality

*Having harvested all the knowledge and
wisdom we can from our mistakes and
failures, we should put them behind us
and go ahead, for vain regretting
interferes with the flow of power into our
own personalities.*

— Edith Johnson

*Persons possessing a pleasing personality
attract success. They turn on others.
Sour souls, know-it-alls, and negative
persons only attract failure and they are
real turn-offs.*

— Napoleon Hill

Day 122

May 3

Pleasing Personality

Make it happen; don't watch it happen.

— Diane R. Vaughn

A Positive Mental Attitude heads the list as the most important trait necessary in developing a Pleasing Personality. Positive is more than merely the opposite of negative. It means having assurance, confidence, a belief in self, a feeling of rightness, and a belief in one's capacity to achieve one's Definite Major Purpose.
— Napoleon Hill

Day 123

Pleasing Personality

There are two ways of spreading light: to be the candle or the mirror that reflects it.

— Edith Wharton

Flexibility consists in the habit of adapting one's self to quickly changing circumstances without losing one's sense of composure or confidence.

— Napoleon Hill

Day 124

May 5

Pleasing Personality

Kindness is always fashionable.

— Amelia E. Barr

Courtesy is the habit of rendering useful service without the expectation of direct reward, the habit of respecting other people's feelings under all circumstances, the habit of going out of one's way if need be to help any less fortunate person whenever possible, and last, but not least, the habit of controlling selfishness, and greed, and envy, and hatred.

— Napoleon Hill

Day 125

Pleasing Personality

As novices, we think we're entirely responsible for the way people treat us. I have long since learned that we are responsible only for the way we treat people.

— *Rose Lane*

People who like people are usually liked by others. People who dislike others generally are not liked by others.

— *Napoleon Hill*

Day 126

May 7

Pleasing Personality

*Of all the things you wear, your expression
is the most important.*

— Janet Lane

*The Habit of Smiling is directly related to
a Positive Mental Attitude. It's a
reflection of faith and joy. If you do not
possess this trait, you should begin
immediately practicing before a mirror.
Smiling and success go together hand in
hand.*

— Napoleon Hill

Day 127

Pleasing Personality

*The best index to a person's character is
(a) how he treats people who can't do him
any good, and (b) how he treats people
who can't fight back.*

— Abigail Van Buren

*Tolerance consists of an open mind on all
subjects, toward all people, at all times.
In addition to being one of the more
important of the traits of a pleasing
personality, an open mind on all subjects
is one of the Twelve Great Riches of Life.*

— Napoleon Hill

Day 128

Pleasing Personality

*You never saw a fish on the wall with its
mouth shut.*

— Sally Berger

*Tactfulness consists in doing and saying
the right thing at the right time.*

— Napoleon Hill

Day 129

Pleasing Personality

We are rich only through what we give;
and poor only through what we refuse and
keep.

— Anne Swetchine

Sincerity begins with you. The woman
who is sincere with others must first be
sincere with herself.

— Napoleon Hill

Day 130

May 11

Pleasing Personality

Civility costs nothing and buys everything.

— Mary Whortley Montague

While we have no tails to wag, our face, with its many muscles and numerous possible shapes, serves as a mirror of one's self, reflecting the inner woman. As such, the smile, the tone of voice, and the expression of the face constitute open windows through which others may see our inner selves.

— Napoleon Hill

Day 131

Pleasing Personality

It is easy to be popular. It is not easy to be just.

— Rose Elizabeth Bird

Women of sound character always have the courage to deal directly and openly with others and they follow this habit even though it may at times be to their disadvantage. However, honesty yields fewer regrets than dishonesty, and it creates a soundness of mind and spirit which comes through the practice of maintaining a clear conscience.

— Napoleon Hill

Day 132

Pleasing Personality

*I didn't belong as a kid, and that always
bothered me. If only I'd known that one
day my differentness would be an asset,
then my early life would have been much
easier.*

— Bette Midler

*Humility of the heart is a sign of great
inner strength and confidence.*

— Napoleon Hill

Day 133

Pleasing Personality

When death, the great reconciler, has come, it is never our tenderness that we repent of, but our severity.

— *George Eliot*

Watch your tongue. It has no mind of its own. Keep it within your cheek and keep your brain in charge of your mouth.

— *Napoleon Hill*

Day 134

May 15

Pleasing Personality

On the banks of the James River, a husband erected a tombstone in memory of his wife, one of those 100 maidens who had come to Virginia in 1619 to marry the lonely settlers. The stone bore this legend: "She touched the soil of Virginia with her little foot and the wilderness became a home."

— Eudora R. Richardson

Life, from birth until death, is dependent to a large degree upon salesmanship.

— Napoleon Hill

Day 135

Pleasing Personality

Every small, positive change we can make in ourselves repays us in confidence in the future.

— Alice Walker

Humor is a sign of faith and is the product of a Positive Mental Attitude. Humor guards one against being overcome by fear and failure. It gives a bounce to life and the human spirit.

— Napoleon Hill

Day 136

Personal Initiative

"There are two types of men," said Andrew Carnegie, "who never amount to anything. One is the fellow who never does anything except that which he is told to do, the other is the fellow who never does more than he is told to do. The man who gets ahead does the thing that should be done without being told to do it, but he does not stop there, he goes the extra mile by doing a great deal more than is expected or demanded of him." Personal Initiative is the power that inspires the completion of that which one begins. It is the power that starts all action. No person is free until he learns to do his own thinking and gains the courage to act on his own Personal Initiative—it is the twin brother of Going the Extra Mile.

Make it happen; don't watch it happen.
— Diane R. Vaughn

Personal Initiative

*Learning is not attained by chance; it
must be sought for with ardor and
attended to with diligence.*

— Abigail Adams

*Personal Initiative bears the same
relationship to an individual that a
self-starter bears to an automobile. It is
the power that inspires the completion of
that which one begins. There are many
starters among women, but there are few
finishers.*

— Napoleon Hill

Day 137

Personal Initiative

The percentage of mistakes in quick decisions is no greater than in long-drawn out vacillations, and the effect of decisiveness itself "makes things go" and creates confidence.

— *Anne O'Hare McCormick*

Personal Initiative reveals favorable opportunities for self-advancement and inspires one to embrace them and realize their full potential.

— *Napoleon Hill*

Day 138

Personal Initiative

*To get anywhere, strike out for somewhere,
or you'll get nowhere.*

— *Martha Lupton*

*Women with Personal Initiative do not
drift aimlessly, but sail boldly out across
the seas of personal success.*

— *Napoleon Hill*

Day 139

May 20

Personal Initiative

It is better to protest than to accept injustice.

— Rosa Parks

Therefore, if you would be done with the negative side of the street then prepare yourself to cross over and begin walking down the avenue named Positive. Move on your Personal Initiative.

— Napoleon Hill

Day 140

Personal Initiative

One sure window into a person's soul is his reading list.

— Mary B. W. Tabor

The mind that has been made ready to receive attracts that which it needs, just as an electromagnet attracts steel filings.

— Napoleon Hill

Day 141

May 22

Personal Initiative

The key to whatever success I enjoy today is: Don't ask. Do.

— Vikki Carr

The most difficult part of any task is that of making a start at performing it.

— Napoleon Hill

Day 142

Personal Initiative

If you don't want to get tackled, don't carry the ball.

— Ann McKay Thompson

Winners are those persons who get in the game and dare to compete for the prize of life's great riches.

— Napoleon Hill

Day 143

May 24

Personal Initiative

You may be disappointed if you fail, but you are doomed if you don't try.

— Beverly Sills

There is always the tendency to wait for a better day or for that moment described as when the "time is right." However, once a start has been made, the power of performance presents itself.

— Napoleon Hill

Day 144

Personal Initiative

Never fear shadows. They simply mean that there's a light somewhere nearby.

— Ruth E. Renkei

Adopt a Definite Major Purpose and see how quickly the habit of moving on your own Personal Initiative will inspire you to action in carrying out the object of your purpose.

— Napoleon Hill

Day 145

Personal Initiative

Too often, the opportunity knocks, but by the time you push back the chain, push back the bolt, unhook the two locks and shut off the burglar alarm, it's too late.

— Rita Coolidge

In conclusion, it should be pointed out once more that few games are ever won by players sitting on the sidelines. If you want to win at life you then must get involved.

— Napoleon Hill

Day 146

Personal Initiative

Opportunities are usually disguised as hard work, so most people don't recognize them.

— Ann Landers

You must be willing to pay the price of success, and that usually can be translated into such terms as: sweat and strain, tears and toil, hope and hurt, brains and brawn.

— Napoleon Hill

Day 147

Personal Initiative

*My mother drew a distinction between
achievement and success. She said,
"Achievement is the knowledge that you
have studied and worked hard and done
the best that is in you. Success is being
praised by others, and that's nice, too, but
not as important or satisfying." Always
aim for achievement and forget about
success.*

— *Helen Hayes*

*Success is reserved for those persons who
are dedicated to the proposition that
achievers are doers and that success comes
to those who are about the business of
succeeding in life.*

— *Napoleon Hill*

Day 148

Personal Initiative

I decided to be a human being and not a role.

— Sonia Johnson

Somewhere along the way you will meet your "other self" face to face – that which can and will carry you over onto the successful side of the street.

— Napoleon Hill

Day 149

May 30

Personal Initiative

To realize originality one has to have the courage to be an amateur.

— Marianne Moore

Never mind how much you know. The important thing is what you can do with what you know!

— Napoleon Hill

Day 150

Personal Initiative

Growth demands a temporary surrender of security.

— Gail Sheehy

Winners are self-starters. They are action-oriented, always taking the initiative. They do not wait on success, but are continually moving in the direction of realizing life goals.

— Napoleon Hill

Day 151

Positive Mental Attitude

Positive Mental Attitude is the right mental attitude in all circumstances. Keep your mind on the things you want and off the things you don't want. Remember the old French proverb: "Be very careful what you set your heart on, for you will surely achieve it." Success attracts more success while failure attracts more failure. This principle presents the means by which the entire philosophy can best be assimilated and put to practical use. You cannot get the most out of the other sixteen principles without understanding and applying this one.

With a Positive Mental Attitude, knowing my shortcomings doesn't bring me down, rather, it helps me to decide what to do about it.
— Marie Hejnal

June 1

Positive Mental Attitude

*The greater part of our happiness or
misery depends upon our dispositions,
and not our circumstances.*

— Martha Washington

Thoughts are powerful.

— Napoleon Hill

Day 152

Positive Mental Attitude

I'm not going to die, I'm going home like a shooting star.

— Sojourner Truth

Ideas can capture the human spirit, move the masses, and turn an entire society about face.

— Napoleon Hill

Day 153

June 3

Positive Mental Attitude

Cheerfulness, if would appear, is a matter which depends fully as much on the state of things within, as on the state of things without and around us.

—*Charlotte Brontë*

Remember: "*As a man thinketh in his heart, so is he.*"

— *Napoleon Hill*

Day 154

Positive Mental Attitude

Why compare yourself to others? No one in the entire world can do a better job than you.

— Susan Carlson

Any woman who takes herself seriously and dares to think the thoughts of personal growth and gain must add the creative catalyst of a Positive Mental Attitude.

— Napoleon Hill

Day 155

June 5

Positive Mental Attitude

I discovered I always have choices and sometimes it's only a choice of attitude.
— Judith M. Knowlton

An attitude can be described as a psychological posture.
— Napoleon Hill

Day 156

Positive Mental Attitude

*One only gets to the top rung on the ladder
by steadily climbing up one at a time, and
suddenly, all sorts of powers, all sorts of
abilities which you thought never
belonged to you—suddenly become within
your own possibility and you think, "Well,
I'll have a go, too."*

— *Margaret Thatcher*

*Self-actualization is an important concept.
Actualization means the transformation of
possibilities into realities.*
*Self-actualization means reaching deep
within yourself and bringing forth your
very best efforts.*

— *Napoleon Hill*

Day 157

June 7

Positive Mental Attitude

An optimist is the human personification of spring.

— Susan J. Bissonette

Behind the concept and reality of self-actualization is a belief in the goodness of "rightness" of life. This is a positive statement and affirms that everyone has a place in life and a right to live life at the fullest.

— Napoleon Hill

Day 158

Positive Mental Attitude

*Life is what we make it. Always has been.
Always will be.*

— Anna Mary (Grandma) Moses

Remember: Thoughts shape our lives!
— Napoleon Hill

Day 159

June 9

Positive Mental Attitude

Life is like a butterfly. You can chase it,
or you can let it come to you.

— Ruth Brown

You can take possession of your thought
power or you can let it be influenced by all
the stray winds of chance and undesirable
circumstances.

— Napoleon Hill

Day 160

Positive Mental Attitude

*Today, see if you can stretch your heart
and expand your love so that it touches
not only those to whom you can give it
easily, but also those who need it so much.*
— *Daphne Rose Kingma*

*Even in the midst of great adversity, the
positive person tells herself over and over
again that life is good and she can
weather the storm.*
— *Napoleon Hill*

Day 161

June 11

Positive Mental Attitude

Kind words are jewels that live in the heart and soul and remain as blessed memories years after they have been spoken.

— Marvea Johnson

The mental in Positive Mental Attitude is the dynamic of thought which provides for the continual reinforcement of the feeling of confidence and belief in one's self.

— Napoleon Hill

Day 162

Positive Mental Attitude

You really have to look inside yourself and find your own inner strength, and say, "I'm proud of what I am and who I am, and I'm just going to be myself."

— *Mariah Carey*

The woman who has a Positive Mental Attitude is one who has assumed a life posture which permits her to confidently face life situations.

— *Napoleon Hill*

Day 163

June 13

Positive Mental Attitude

Optimism is what you do, how you live.
— Andrea Dworkin

Our beliefs must be continually reinforced. The muscles of self-confidence must be strengthened through a daily work-out, mental in design, so that in the midst of adversity one will be strong enough to win in spite of the odds.
— Napoleon Hill

Day 164

Positive Mental Attitude

The accumulation of small, optimistic acts produces quality in our culture and in your life. Our culture resonates in tense times to individual acts of grace.

— *Jennifer James*

Peace of mind can only be obtained through a Positive Mental Attitude. Peace of mind requires helping others to help themselves.

— *Napoleon Hill*

Day 165

June 15

Positive Mental Attitude

Character contributes to beauty. It fortifies a woman as her youth fades. A mode of conduct, a standard of courage, discipline, fortitude, and integrity can do a great deal to make a woman beautiful.
— Jacqueline Bisset

A Positive Mental Attitude is the first and the most important step we must take in the control and direction of our minds since all degrees of a negative mental attitude leave us wide open to every negative influence we contact.
— Napoleon Hill

Day 166

Positive Mental Attitude

Perseverance is failing nineteen times and succeeding the twentieth.

— Julie Andrews

You can develop a Positive Mental Attitude by selecting a pace-maker, and emulating her.

— Napoleon Hill

Day 167

June 17

Positive Mental Attitude

Courage is the atom of change.
> *— Jacqueline Bisset*

It is important to realize that the great crime of the universe is stagnation.
> *— Napoleon Hill*

Day 168

Positive Mental Attitude

*Nobody really cares if you are miserable,
so you might as well be happy.*

— Cythina Nelms

*Positive Mental Attitude is the only
condition of the mind in which we can
express Applied Faith and draw upon the
forces of Infinite Intelligence.*

— Napoleon Hill

Day 169

June 19

Positive Mental Attitude

A strong, positive self-image is the best possible preparation for success.

> — *Dr. Joyce Brothers*

Positive Mental Attitude is the only condition which permits us to get on the Success Beam.

> — *Napoleon Hill*

Day 170

Positive Mental Attitude

Invest in the human soul. Who knows, it might be a diamond in the rough.

— Mary McLeod Bethune

Positive Mental Attitude is the only condition of the mind in which we can meet and recognize our "other self" – that self which has no limitations.

— Napoleon Hill

Day 171

June 21

Positive Mental Attitude

Be on the alert to recognize your prime at whatever time of life it may occur.

— Muriel Spark

The woman who has a Positive Mental Attitude is one who has assumed a life posture which permits her to confidently face life situations.

— Napoleon Hill

Day 172

Positive Mental Attitude

Look at everything as though you were seeing it either for the first or last time. Then your time on earth will be filled with glory.

— *Betty Smith*

To maintain the feeling of confidence, there must be repetitious thought charged with assurance and belief itself.

— *Napoleon Hill*

Day 173

June 23

Positive Mental Attitude

I'm looking forward to looking back on all this.

— Sandra Knell

Even in the midst of great adversity, the positive person tells herself, over and over again that life is good and she can weather the storm.

— Napoleon Hill

Day 174

Positive Mental Attitude

Beauty is in the eye of the beholder.
        — Margaret Wolfe Hungerford

It is the believing woman who achieves.
        — Napoleon Hill

Day 175

June 25

Positive Mental Attitude

Stinky attitudes are airborne. They waft around and add to the pollution on planet earth. But we don't have to take a deep breath to detect attitudes; they're as obvious as a new pair of iridescent sneakers. Just as surely as we wear our Liz Claibornes and Ralph Laurens, we can be seen strutting, sneaking, and slumping around in our negative 'tudes.

— Patsy Clairmont

You can form the habit of tolerance and keep an open mind on all subjects, toward people of all races and creeds, and learn to like people as they are instead of demanding them to be like you.

— Napoleon Hill

Day 176

Positive Mental Attitude

There are so many things that we wish we had done yesterday, so few that we feel like doing today.

— Mignon McLaughlin

Winners are those persons in life who have taken possession of their minds, exercise control over their thoughts and maintain a Positive Mental Attitude in their quest for success.

— Napoleon Hill

Day 177

June 27

Positive Mental Attitude

A strong positive attitude will create more miracles than any wonder drug.

— *Patricia Neal*

You can take possession of your thought power or you can let it be influenced by all the stray winds of chance and undesirable circumstances.

— *Napoleon Hill*

Day 178

Positive Mental Attitude

My motto is that I enjoy life. I think there's a kind of simplicity to that way of thinking.

— Jenna Elfman

A Positive Mental Attitude is generated when a person assumes a confident life-stance which originates and is sustained through the control of one's thoughts.

— Napoleon Hill

Day 179

Positive Mental Attitude

The only difference between a rut and a grave is their dimensions.

— Ellen Glasgow

Keep your mind on the things you want and off the things you don't want. Remember the old French proverb: "Be very careful what you set your heart on, for you will surely achieve it."

— Napoleon Hill

Day 180

Positive Mental Attitude

Humility is not my forte, and whenever I dwell for any length of time on my own shortcomings, they gradually begin to seem mild, harmless, rather engaging little things, not at all like the staring defects in other people's characters.

— *Margaret Halsey*

Adjust yourself to other people's states of mind and their peculiarities so as to get along peacefully with them, and refrain from taking notice of trivial circumstances in your human relations by refusing to allow them to become controversial incidents.

— *Napoleon Hill*

Day 181

Enthusiasm

Enthusiasm is faith in action. Enthusiasm comes from the Greek words "en" which means "in" and "theos" which means "God." It is the intense emotion known as burning desire. Enthusiasm comes from within, although it radiates outwardly in the expression of one's voice and countenance. Enthusiasm is power because it is the instrument by which adversities and failures and temporary defeats may be transmuted into action backed by faith. The flame of enthusiasm burning within you turns thought into action.

No longer do I have to accept or compromise with less than my own personal expectations.
— Deanna Davis

July 1

Enthusiasm

The essence of pleasure is spontaneity.
— *Germaine Greer*

Enthusiasm causes one to glow with self-confidence.
— *Napoleon Hill*

Day 182

Enthusiasm

Life itself is the proper binge.

— Julia Child

Enthusiasm definitely takes the drudgery out of labor.

— Napoleon Hill

Day 183

Enthusiasm

The sense of the word among the Greeks
affords the noblest definition of it;
enthusiasm signifies "God in us."
— Madame de Stael

Enthusiasm is the utilization of the God
within you and the ability to tap and
direct this tremendous force.
— Napoleon Hill

Day 184

Enthusiasm

*It's easier to act your way into new ways of
feeling than to feel yourself into new ways
of acting.*

— *Susan Glaser*

*Remember, you are developing the habit of
Controlled Enthusiasm and the creation
of habits requires repetition through
physical action.*

— *Napoleon Hill*

Day 185

July 5

Enthusiasm

You will do foolish things, but do them with enthusiasm.

— Colette

Enthusiasm steps up thought vibrations and stimulates the imagination.

— Napoleon Hill

Day 186

Enthusiasm

It isn't the great pleasures that count the most; it's making a great deal out of the little ones.

— *Jean Webster*

Enthusiasm gives a thrust to life, an impetus toward success.

— *Napoleon Hill*

Day 187

July 7

Enthusiasm

Each dawn holds a new hope for a new plan, making the start of each day the start of a new life.

— Gina Blair

Enthusiasm concentrates the powers of the mind and gives them the wings of action.

— Napoleon Hill

Day 188

Enthusiasm

Deep listening from the heart is one half of true communication. Speaking from the heart is the other half.

— Sandra Paddison

Enthusiasm gives brilliance and color to the spoken word.

— Napoleon Hill

Day 189

Enthusiasm

*My heart is singing for joy this morning.
A miracle has happened! The light of
understanding has shone upon my little
pupil's mind, and behold, all things are
changed!*

— Annie Sullivan

*Enthusiasm is power, because it is the
instrument by which adversities and
failures and temporary defeat may be
transmuted into action backed by faith.*

— Napoleon Hill

Day 190

Enthusiasm

The real power behind whatever success I have now was something I found within myself—something that's in all of us, I think, a little piece of God just waiting to be discovered.

— *Tina Turner*

Enthusiasm is "faith in action," pushing aside those obstacles which stand between a woman and her Definite Major Purpose.

— *Napoleon Hill*

Day 191

July 11

Enthusiasm

*We've stopped counting fireflies at dusk,
standing naked in the rain, finger painting
with our feet and stuffing a bag full of
costumes and making our "poet's corner" in
the backyard, with lanterns and tents made
out of chenille bedspreads. We deserve to be
the caretakers for our spirits and dreams,
and this means truly sensing and listening
for our most alive route.*

— Sark

*Enthusiasm moves mountains, blows
apart negative thoughts, repels the
negativism of others, secures support for
your ideas, enlists the cooperation of
others, encourages confidence, and
underscores your sincerity of purpose.*

— Napoleon Hill

Day 192

Enthusiasm

Light tomorrow with today.
> — *Elizabeth Barrett Browning*

Give a woman a burning desire to achieve a definite end, and a definite motive setting fire to that desire and very quickly the flames of enthusiasm will begin burning and a power will be generated which, when properly directed, will assist a person in realizing their Definite Major Purpose.
> — *Napoleon Hill*

Day 193

July 13

Enthusiasm

The bravest thing you can do when you are not brave is to profess courage and act accordingly.

— Corra Harris

Enthusiasm clears the mind of negative cobwebs and prepares the way for the "faith in action" so vital to personal success.

— Napoleon Hill

Day 194

Enthusiasm

To look backward for a while is to refresh the eye, to restore it, and to render it more fit for its prime function of looking forward.

— *Margaret Fairless Barber*

Remember, enthusiasm thrives on a positive spirit.

— *Napoleon Hill*

Day 195

July 15

Enthusiasm

If you want to touch the other shore badly enough, barring an impossible situation, you will. If your desire is diluted for any reason, you'll never make it.

— *Dina Nyad*

Enthusiasm is the "action factor of thought!" Where it is strong enough, it literally forces one into action appropriate to the nature of the motive which inspired it.

— *Napoleon Hill*

Day 196

Teamwork

Teamwork is harmonious cooperation that is willing, voluntary and free. Whenever the spirit of Teamwork is the dominating influence in business or industry, success is inevitable. Harmonious cooperation is a priceless asset that you can acquire in proportion to your giving. Teamwork, in a spirit of friendliness, costs little in the way of time and effort. Generosity, fair treatment, courtesy, and a willingness to serve are qualities that pay high dividends whenever they are applied in human relations.

If I failed to successfully accomplish my responsibilities, I prevented those who followed me from accomplishing their duties.
— Dr. Judith B. Arcy

Teamwork

*Imparting knowledge is only lighting
other men's candles at our lamp, without
depriving ourselves of any flame.*

— Jane Porter

*Cooperation, like love and friendship, is
something one receives by giving.*

— Napoleon Hill

Day 197

Teamwork

A clay pot sitting in the sun will always be a clay pot. It has to go through the white heat of the furnace to become porcelain.
— *Mildred Stouven*

Underdogs can become winners when they believe themselves capable of winning and are willing to commit themselves to victory.
— *Napoleon Hill*

Day 198

July 18

Teamwork

*When people universally realize that all are
united by the common bond of mortality and
by the basic needs . . . the need to worship
and to love, to be housed and fed, to work and
play, perhaps we will have learned to
understand, which is to love spiritually, and
there will be peace and brotherhood on earth.
Without brotherhood, peace is not possible.*
— *Faith Baldwin*

*Not only does your present and future
depend upon your ability to join hands
with others – but the tomorrow our
children will know will depend upon how
willing we are to walk the road of life
together in peace and prosperity as we
build a better world.*
— *Napoleon Hill*

Day 199

Teamwork

*Our happiness is greatest when we
contribute to the happiness of others.*

— *Harriet Shepard*

*The cooperative spirit is a gift which can
be offered to another human being.*

— *Napoleon Hill*

Day 200

Teamwork

*Remember, we all stumble, every one of us.
That's why it's a comfort to go hand in
hand.*

— *Emily Kimbrough*

*The cooperative spirit is also a torch
which can be passed on to another
generation, holding high the light of hope
and love, peace and prosperity.*

— *Napoleon Hill*

Day 201

Teamwork

Surround yourself only with people who are going to lift you higher.

— *Oprah Winfrey*

A cooperative spirit increases your success potential while benefiting others.

— *Napoleon Hill*

Day 202

Teamwork

If I had to characterize one quality as the genius of feminist thought, culture, and action, it would be the connectivity.

— *Robin Morgan*

We are not only surrounded by the water of humanity, but we are connected and joined together by common concerns, interests and needs which bind us and create the very ground of our being and the human experience.

— *Napoleon Hill*

Day 203

Teamwork

Reinforce the stitch that ties us, and I will do the same for you.

— Doris Schwerin

A contagious enthusiasm is required if a group is to become "fired-up" and prepared for victory.

— Napoleon Hill

Day 204

July 24

Teamwork

Treat your friends as you do your best pictures, and place them in their best light.

— Jennie Jerome Churchill

Winners win because they believe winning possible.

— Napoleon Hill

Day 205

Teamwork

Never refuse any advance of friendship,
for if nine out of ten bring you nothing,
one alone may repay you.

> — *Madame de Tencin*

Willing teamwork is the only type that
leads to constructive ends, the only type
that sustains the power of people through
coordinated efforts.

> — *Napoleon Hill*

Day 206

Teamwork

Continuous effort—not strength or intelligence—is the key to unlocking our potential.

— Liane Cardes

Teamwork produces power, but the question as to whether the power is temporary or permanent depends upon the motive that inspires the cooperation.

— Napoleon Hill

Day 207

Teamwork

What we plan we build.

— Phoebe Cary

Victory, if it is to be realized, requires team effort – teamwork.

— Napoleon Hill

Day 208

Teamwork

Of any stopping place in life, it is good to ask whether it will be a good place from which to go on as well as a good place to remain.

— *Mary Catherine Bateson*

The individual attempting to win at life or the organization attempting to realize great gains needs to understand the reality of momentum.

— *Napoleon Hill*

Day 209

Teamwork

Unless you know what you want, you can't ask for it.

— Jeanne Segal, Ph.D.

In the life of every woman or any organization, there are times when an added power is needed to carry on through seeming failure to the point of victory.

— Napoleon Hill

Day 210

Teamwork

Always have some project underway . . .
an ongoing project that goes over from day
to day and thus makes each day a small
unit of time.

— Dr. Lillian Troll

Great physical power can be produced by
coordination of efforts but the endurance
of that power – its quality, scope, and
strength are taken from that intangible
something known as the "spirit" in which
people work together for the attainment of
a common goal.

— Napoleon Hill

Day 211

Teamwork

It is not fair to ask of others what you are not willing to do yourself.

— *Eleanor Roosevelt*

It's a wise woman who understands that there is strength in numbers and integrity through unity.

— *Napoleon Hill*

Day 212

Self-Discipline

Self-Discipline means taking possession of your own mind. Self-Discipline begins with the mastery of thought. If you do not control your thoughts, you cannot control your needs. Self-Discipline calls for a balancing of the emotions of your heart with the reasoning faculty of your head. It is the bottleneck through which all of your personal power for success must flow. Direct your thoughts, control your emotions, and ordain your destiny. As our culture has become more complex, the need for self-control has increased.

I can never lose sight of what it is that I want to pursue if I always take possession of my own reasoning and thoughts.
— Wilma Jackson

August 1

Self-Discipline

As tools become rusty, so does the mind; a garden uncared for soon becomes smothered in weeds; a talent neglected withers and dies.

— Ethel R. Page

People who keep on winning in life are those who are willing to pay the price of success in terms of developing and maintaining constructive, success-producing habits.

— Napoleon Hill

Day 213

Self-Discipline

We are always afraid to start something that we want to make very good, true, and serious.

— Brenda Ueland

Self-discipline means taking possession of your own mind.

— Napoleon Hill

Day 214

August 3

Self-Discipline

*I believe in hard work. It keeps the
wrinkles out of the mind and the spirit.*
                                — *Helena Rubinstein*

*What you are as a person, whether it be
success or failure, depends to a large
degree upon your personal habits.*
                                — *Napoleon Hill*

Day 215

Self-Discipline

Self-restraint may be alien to the human temperament, but humanity without restraint will dig its own grave.
> — *Marya Mannes*

You can choose to create within you habits that are success-producing.
> — *Napoleon Hill*

Day 216

August 5

Self-Discipline

There are two ways to meet difficulties.
You alter the difficulties or you alter
yourself to meet them.

— Phyliss Bottome

The most important habits are those
which have to do with the thoughts you
think.

— Napoleon Hill

Day 217

Self-Discipline

You have to learn the rules of the game.
And then, you have to play better than
anyone else.

— Dianne Feinstein

It doesn't take too long to realize that what
a woman thinks is translated into
physical terms with regard to what she
does and achieves in life.

— Napoleon Hill

Day 218

August 7

Self-Discipline

*In the end, we are all the sum total of our actions.
Character cannot be counterfeited, nor can it be
put on and cast off as if it were a garment to meet
the whim of the moment. Like the markings on
wood which are ingrained in the very heart of
the tree, character requires time and nurture for
growth and development. Thus also, day by day,
we write our own destiny; for inexorably we
become what we do. This I believe, is the
supreme logic and the law of life.*
— *Madame Chiang Kai-shek*

*When you have gained control over your
thought habits, you will have come a long
way in realizing the type of Self-Discipline
that speeds up the success process.*
— *Napoleon Hill*

Day 219

Self-Discipline

He who angers you, conquers you.

— Elizabeth Kenny

As a rule of thumb, keep your plans to yourself.

— Napoleon Hill

Day 220

August 9

Self-Discipline

*What really matters is what you do with
what you have.*

— Shirley Lord

*Shoot for the stars! It may not be in the
best taste for you to over-shoot your
abilities in terms of personal ambition,
but it is a lot better than setting an easily
obtainable goal which requires little effort.*
— Napoleon Hill

Day 221

Self-Discipline

*No one can avoid aging, but aging
productively is something else.*
> — *Katharine Graham*

*If you aim at a very big achievement and
only obtain a moderate achievement, you
still have realized a goal of great value.*
> — *Napoleon Hill*

Day 222

August 11

Self-Discipline

And remember this: if you think you're too small to be effective – you've never been in bed with a mosquito.

— Anita Roddick

If you allow yourself to be held back in the beginning, you will have only sold yourself short.

— Napoleon Hill

Day 223

Self-Discipline

All serious daring starts from within.

— Eudora Welty

Self-discipline represents the "bottleneck" through which the great power within this Science must pass.

— Napoleon Hill

Day 224

August 13

Self-Discipline

Challenges make you discover things about yourself that you never really knew. They're what make the instrument stretch—what makes you go beyond the norm.

— Cicely Tyson

Self-discipline is a quality/habit you should persistently apply as it grows stronger with the passing of time and moves you ever closer to success.

— Napoleon Hill

Day 225

Self-Discipline

Even though you may want to move forward in your life, you may have one foot on the brakes. In order to be free, we must learn how to let go.

> — *Mary Manin Morrissey*

Adopt the motto: "Deeds not words." Let your actions talk for you.

> — *Napoleon Hill*

Day 226

August 15

Self-Discipline

When people keep telling you that you can't do a thing, you kind of like to try it.
— *Margaret Chase*

You will find a lot more people willing to tear you down by discouragement than you will find flattering you and building up your ego. Of course, the best way to avoid such discouragement is to confide in no one but those who have a genuine sympathy with your cause and an understanding of life's great possibilities.
— *Napoleon Hill*

Day 227

Learning from Adversity and Defeat

Every adversity carries with it the seed of an equivalent or greater benefit. Individual success usually is in exact proportion to the scope of the defeat the individual has experienced and mastered. Most so-called failures represent only a temporary defeat that may prove to be a blessing in disguise. Defeat is never the same as failure unless and until it has been accepted as such.

Isn't it interesting how your life, and all you have planned for, can change in an instant?
— Betsy Carlson

August 16

Learning from Adversity and Defeat

If we had no winter, the spring would not be so pleasant; if we did not sometimes taste of adversity, prosperity would not be so welcome.

— Anne Bradstreet

Every adversity carries with it the seed of an equivalent or a greater benefit provided you look for it.

— Napoleon Hill

Day 228

Learning from Adversity and Defeat

*Mistakes are a fact of life. It is the
response to error that counts.*

— Nikki Giovanni

*Most so-called failures only represent
temporary setbacks which can prove to be
blessings in disguise.*

— Napoleon Hill

Day 229

August 18

Learning from Adversity and Defeat

Between two evils, I always pick the one I never tried before.

> — *Mae West*

Women who learn from adversity discover the great pearls of the good life.

> — *Napoleon Hill*

Day 230

Learning from Adversity and Defeat

*The Slave knows that life is in essence
unpredictable.*

— *Rebecca West*

*Keep in mind that defeat is but a
temporary state of affairs unless you
choose to accept it as final.*

— *Napoleon Hill*

Day 231

August 20
Learning from Adversity and Defeat

Don't compromise yourself. You're all you got.

> — *Janis Joplin*

If we examine the records, we shall be convinced that those women who attain success are those who have adopted the habit of accepting defeat as nothing but an urge to greater effort.

> — *Napoleon Hill*

Day 232

Learning from Adversity and Defeat

I'm not afraid of storms for I'm learning how to sail my ship.

— Louisa May Alcott

Time eventually corrects all evils, rights all wrongs for those who realize that adversity is one of the great teachers of life.

— Napoleon Hill

Day 233

August 22
Learning from Adversity and Defeat

*I have never been one who thought that
the Lord should make life easy; I've just
asked Him to make me strong.*
— *Eva Bowring*

*Defeat may lead to the development of a
stronger will-power, provided one accepts
it as a challenge to greater effort and not
as a signal to stop trying.*
— *Napoleon Hill*

Day 234

Learning from Adversity and Defeat

You may have a fresh start any moment you choose, for this thing that we call "failure" is not the falling down, but the staying down.

— *Mary Pickford*

Defeat may cause one to acquire the habit of taking self-inventory for the purpose of uncovering weaknesses responsible for the defeat.

— *Napoleon Hill*

Day 235

August 24
Learning from Adversity and Defeat

Reality is something you rise above.

> *— Liza Minnelli*

Learning from adversity is a part of the great system of natural laws designed by an all-wise Creator to protect woman against her own follies, save her from her own mistakes, and insure her against self-destruction.

> *— Napoleon Hill*

Day 236

Learning from Adversity and Defeat

No soul that aspires can ever fail to rise;
no heart that loves can ever be abandoned.
Difficulties exist only that in overcoming
them we may grow strong.

— Annie Besant

Coming to grips with this principle could
produce a critical turning point in your
life.

— Napoleon Hill

Day 237

August 26
Learning from Adversity and Defeat

*I'll say this for adversity: people seem to
be able to stand it, and that's more than I
can say for prosperity.*

— *Kim Hubbard*

*The woman who "fails and still fights"
usually has uncovered a source of Creative
Vision enabling her to convert temporary
defeat into permanent success.*

— *Napoleon Hill*

Day 238

Learning from Adversity and Defeat

People fail forward to success.

— Mary Kay Ash

We shall find that the individual success usually is in exact proportion to the scope of the defeat the individual has experienced and mastered.

— Napoleon Hill

Day 239

August 28
Learning from Adversity and Defeat

*The greatest mistake you can make in life
is to be continually fearing that you will
make one.*

— Ellen Hubbard

*Often defeat breaks up some negative
habits one has formed, thus releasing
energies for a new start through the
development of more positive habits.*

— Napoleon Hill

Day 240

Learning from Adversity and Defeat

. . . Most turning points are evident only afterward, when the fact that had to have been there is revealed.

— Amanda Cross

The compensating benefits of failure and defeat often cannot be seen or recognized as benefits until one looks backward at the experiences after a sufficient lapse of time.

— Napoleon Hill

Day 241

August 30

Learning from Adversity and Defeat

*Don't fight the waves. Dive under, bob up,
or catch the curl and ride the wave. The
ocean is stronger than you: you might as
well be a matchstick in comparison. But
if you yield to the waves, they carry you,
their power becomes you.*
— Elizabeth Cunningham

*The person who can go through defeat
which crushes the finer emotions, and still
avoid having her inner soul smothered by
the experience may become a master in her
chosen field of endeavor.*
— Napoleon Hill

Day 242

Learning from Adversity and Defeat

*When you get into a tight place and
everything goes against you, 'til it seems
as though you could not hold on a minute
longer, never give up then, for that is just
the place and time that the tide will turn.*
— *Harriet Beecher Stowe*

*It is crucial to note that the turning point
at which one begins to attain success in
the higher brackets of achievement usually
is marked by some form of outstanding
defeat or failure.*

— *Napoleon Hill*

Day 243

Controlled Attention

Controlled Attention leads to mastery in any type of human endeavor, because it enables one to focus the powers of his mind upon the attainment of a definite objective and to keep it so directed at will. Great achievements come from minds that are at peace with themselves. Peace within one's mind is not a matter of luck, but is a priceless possession, which can be attained only by Self-Discipline based upon Controlled Attention. Concentration on one's major purpose projects a clear picture of that purpose upon the conscious mind and holds it there until it is taken over by the subconscious mind and acted upon.

I enjoy being challenged, and I strive to seek out the impossible in order to prove that <u>impossible</u> becomes the <u>possible</u> when I enter the situation with a focused mind and a clear vision of the purpose.

— Carol Macinga

September 1

Controlled Attention

Only when I make room for the child's voice within me do I feel genuine and creative.

— Alice Miller

The mind never remains inactive. It works continuously, reacting to those influences which reach it.

— Napoleon Hill

Day 244

Controlled Attention

Listening creates holy silence. Listening is like the rain.

— Rachel Naomi Remen

Controlled Attention is an absolute prerequisite if one is to tap into the great reservoir of power with Infinite Intelligence.

— Napoleon Hill

Day 245

September 3
Controlled Attention

*We ought to be able to learn some things
secondhand. There is not enough time for
us to make all the mistakes ourselves.*

— Harriet Hall

*Controlled Attention is the highest form of
Self-Discipline.*

— Napoleon Hill

Controlled Attention

Power is the ability to do good things for others.

— Brooke Astor

Great achievements come from minds which are at peace with themselves and to those who are at peace with others.

— Napoleon Hill

Day 247

September 5

Controlled Attention

*Old fashioned ways which no longer apply
to changed conditions are a snare in
which the feet of women have always
become readily entangled.*

— *Jane Addams*

*The difference between Controlled Attention
and casual attention is very great. It
amounts to a difference between feeding the
mind on thought material which will
produce that which one desires, and
allowing the mind through neglect to feed
upon the type of garbage that will produce
that which one most fears and least desires.*
— *Napoleon Hill*

Day 248

Controlled Attention

You need to claim the events of your life to make yourself yours. When you truly possess all that you have been and done, which may take some time, you are fierce with reality.

— Florida Scott-Maxwell

Controlled Attention, when it is focused upon the object of one's Definite Major Purpose, is the medium by which one makes positive application of the principle and process of autosuggestion.

— Napoleon Hill

Day 249

September 7
Controlled Attention

Risk! Risk anything! Care no more for the opinions of others. Do the hardest thing on earth for you. Act for yourself. Face the truth.

— Katherine Mansfield

Keep your mind on the things you want and off the things you don't want.

— Napoleon Hill

Day 250

Controlled Attention

She had nothing to fall back on: not maleness, not whiteness, not ladyhood, not anything. And out of the profound desolation of her reality she may well have invented herself.

— Toni Morrison

A good example is a person whose thoughts are fixed upon failure and poverty. Through autosuggestion such thoughts as "I'm a loser" or "I'll never have anything" are transferred to the subconscious mind, fed back into the conscious mind and are expressed as actions which guarantee that the person will lose and have little in life.

— Napoleon Hill

Day 251

September 9

Controlled Attention

Show me how you follow your deepest desires, spiraling down into the ache with the ache, and I will show you how I reach inward and open outward to feel the kiss of the Mystery, sweet lips on my own, every day.

— *Oriah Mountain Dreamer*

It is obvious that when one voluntarily fixes her attention upon a Definite Major Purpose of a positive nature, and forces her mind to dwell on that purpose, that she "conditions" her mind to act upon that purpose.

— *Napoleon Hill*

Day 252

Controlled Attention

There is no point at which you can say,
"Well, I am successful now. I might as
well take a nap."

— Carrie Fisher

Controlled Attention may be compared to
a gardener who keeps her fertile garden
spot cleared of weeds so that it may yield a
bountiful harvest of edible foods.

— Napoleon Hill

Day 253

September 11
Controlled Attention

Maybe being oneself is always an acquired taste.

— Patricia Hampl

Controlled Attention is self-mastery of the highest order. It reflects organized mind-power. Actually, Controlled Attention and Self-Discipline are so closely related that they can be best described as "twin brothers."

— Napoleon Hill

Day 254

Controlled Attention

*No one is so eager to gain new experience
as he who doesn't know how to make use
of the old ones.*

— Marie Ebner von Eshenbach

*One either takes possession of her own
mind and directs it to the attainment of
that which she desires or her mind takes
possession of her and gives her whatever
the circumstances of life hand out.*

— Napoleon Hill

Day 255

September 13
Controlled Attention

I must govern the clock, not be governed by it.

— *Golda Meir*

Perhaps you can better understand how the principle of Controlled Attention works if you realize that one can control the span and object of attention by thinking of it, talking of it, eating it, drinking it, sleeping and dreaming it and thus making it a twenty-four hour obsession.

— *Napoleon Hill*

Day 256

Controlled Attention

The funny thing about going after success in any venture is that there is no failure as long as you pay attention to your results.

— *Barrie Dolnick*

Controlled Attention is the act of focusing the mind upon a given desire until the ways and means for its realization have been worked out and successfully put into operation.

— *Napoleon Hill*

Day 257

September 15
Controlled Attention

*Thinkers rule the world. They always
have and they always will. All people
think, but the tragedy of life is that so few
of us think creatively or constructively; so
few recognize the fact that thought is a
creative force.*

— *Venice Bloodworth*

*Success in all the higher brackets of
individual achievement is attained only
by the application of thought power,
properly organized and directed to definite
ends.*

— *Napoleon Hill*

Day 258

Accurate Thinking

The power of thought is the most dangerous or the most beneficial power available to man, depending, of course, upon how it is used. Through the power of thought man builds great empires of civilization. Through the same power other people trample down empires as if they were helpless clay. Thought is the only thing over which man has been given the complete privilege of control. The Accurate Thinker always submits his emotional desires and decisions to his head for judiciary examination before he relies upon them as being sound, for he knows that his head is more dependable than his heart. The accurate thinker separates facts from fiction and separates facts into two classes: important and unimportant.

Accurate Thinking is a skill that will get you what you want. Many people get caught up in the action steps or the mechanics of how to go about getting something they want. In reality, the key to achieving a goal is your commitment and your intention.

— Kathy Quinlan Perez

September 16
Accurate Thinking

The first problem for all of us, man and woman, is not to learn, but to unlearn.

— Gloria Steinem

An accurate thinker sees both the way and the doing of the way.

— Napoleon Hill

Day 259

Accurate Thinking

I'm not sure I want popular opinion on my side – I've noticed those with the most opinions often have the fewest facts.

— Bethania McKenstry

Accurate thinking is a grasping for conclusion through intuition after all of the possibilities within a given situation have been explored.

— Napoleon Hill

Day 260

September 18
Accurate Thinking

Today, if you are not confused, you're just not thinking clearly.

— Irene Peter

Remember, the accurate thinker is one who can state a problem simply, clearly, and precisely.

— Napoleon Hill

Day 261

Accurate Thinking

Action without study is fatal.
Study without action is futile.

— Mary Beard

Don't tackle a problem with a closed mind.

— Napoleon Hill

Day 262

September 20
Accurate Thinking

Think wrongly if you please, but in all cases think for yourself.

— *Doris Lessing*

The accurate thinker is always concerned that the decisions reached and applied are consistent with one's life goals or Definite Major Purpose.

— *Napoleon Hill*

Day 263

Accurate Thinking

The person who knows how will always have a job. The person who knows why will always be his boss.

— *Diane Ravitch*

Each decision you reach, each step you take, ought to draw you closer to realizing your Definite Major Purpose.

— *Napoleon Hill*

Day 264

September 22

Accurate Thinking

Once you wake up thought in a man, you can never put it to sleep again.

— *Zora Neale Hurston*

Be patient. Be courageous. You can find your way out of the maze – a conclusion, a solution awaits you as an accurate thinker.

— *Napoleon Hill*

Day 265

Accurate Thinking

Expecting life to treat you well because you are a good person is like expecting an angry bull not to charge because you are a vegetarian.

— *Shari R. Barr*

There is no substitute for precise thinking.
— *Napoleon Hill*

Day 266

September 24
Accurate Thinking

Let us be of good cheer, remembering that the misfortunes hardest to bear are those which never come.

— Amy Lowell

Stop trying to think out your problems alone and begin using the knowledge and experience and judgment of others.

— Napoleon Hill

Day 267

Accurate Thinking

Never give up and never face the facts.
— Ruth Gordon

If the circumstances of your life are not to your liking, you may change them by changing your mental attitude to conform with the circumstances you desire.
— Napoleon Hill

Day 268

September 26
Accurate Thinking

The objective is not to pass, but to surpass.
— Millie Thornton

The habit of accurate, organized thinking pays off. There is no limit to the amount it pays when put into intelligent action, except the mental limitations which you set up in your own mind.
— Napoleon Hill

Day 269

Accurate Thinking

*Where I was born, and how I lived is
unimportant. It is what I have done and
where I have been that should be of
interest.*

— *Georgia O'Keeffe*

*Next to life itself, the greatest miracle
known to man is the miracle of thought,
and no small part of this miracle consists
in the amazing simplicity with which so
complicated a mechanism as the brain
can be operated by the power of will.*

— *Napoleon Hill*

Day 270

September 28
Accurate Thinking

It is best to learn as we go, not go as we have learned.

— *Leslie Jeanne Sahler*

There can be no fixed price on the value of organized thinking! But there is no power in thought until it is organized and directed toward a definite end and implemented by intelligent action.

— *Napoleon Hill*

Day 271

Accurate Thinking

A closed mind is a dying mind.

— Edna Ferber

*"The first fact one must recognize," said
Andrew Carnegie, "in order to become an
accurate thinker, is the fact that the power
with which one thinks is mental dynamite
which can be organized and used
constructively for the attainment of definite
ends; but if not controlled and directed, it
may become a mental explosive that will
literally blast your hopes of achievement and
lead to inevitable failure."*

— Napoleon Hill

Day 272

September 30

Accurate Thinking

Well, maybe there is no profit on each individual jar, but we'll make it up in volume.

— Lucy Ricardo

The person who can accurately think through situations related to one's Definite Major Purpose is a craftsman and rises quickly to an enviable position.

— Napoleon Hill

Day 273

Maintenance of Sound Health

The mind and the body are so closely related that whatever one does affects the other. One does not enjoy sound health without a health consciousness. Sound health begins with a sound health consciousness, just as financial success begins with a prosperity consciousness. To maintain a health consciousness, one must think in terms of sound health, not in terms of illness and disease. As the old sayings go: "You have nothing if you do not have your health" and "If you think you're sick, you are."

In order for us to remain healthy, both physically and emotionally, we must continue to stimulate ourselves with a healthy conscience and maintain a balance between body and mind.

— Patsi Gately

October 1

Maintenance of Sound Health

Health is not a condition of matter, but of mind, nor can the material senses bear reliable testimony on the subject of health.
— *Mary Baker Eddy*

If you think you are sick, you are.
— *Napoleon Hill*

Day 274

Maintenance of Sound Health

Bodies never lie.

— Agnes DeMille

We cannot separate the body and the mind, for they are one.

— Napoleon Hill

Day 275

October 3

Maintenance of Sound Health

We have no right to look for a happy old age if, in our living, we habitually violate physical and spiritual laws. The full blessing of length of days comes to those who have known how to live, and the beauty of the years of maturity can be assured only by maintaining high standards of living.

— *Janet Baird*

A change in mental attitude often aids in the development of bodily resistance against disease.

— *Napoleon Hill*

Day 276

Maintenance of Sound Health

The more man follows nature and is obedient to her laws, the longer he will live; the further he deviates from these, the shorter will be his existence. Health is nature's reward for getting into harmony with her laws.

— *Anita Hesselgesser*

We are not only one in the sense of a mind-body, but we are also part of the environment in which we live.

— *Napoleon Hill*

Day 277

October 5

Maintenance of Sound Health

*Humor is an excellent path to
enlightenment.*

> *— Tama Stark*

*The key to good health is a physically fit
body complemented by a Positive Mental
Attitude which is expressed as a positive
approach to life.*

> *— Napoleon Hill*

Day 278

Maintenance of Sound Health

There is a rainbow in you stronger than steel.

— Megan Doherty

Don't forget to express gratitude daily, by prayer and affirmation, for the blessings you have.

— Napoleon Hill

Day 279

October 7

Maintenance of Sound Health

Fortunately, psychoanalysis is not the only way to resolve inner conflicts. Life itself remains a very effective therapist.

— *Karen Horney*

Success comes to those who are physically and mentally fit.

— *Napoleon Hill*

Day 280

Maintenance of Sound Health

As I grow older, part of my emotional survival plan must be to actively seek inspiration instead of passively waiting for it to find me.

— Bebe Moore Campbell

Don't neglect to play and relax regularly.

— Napoleon Hill

Day 281

October 9

Maintenance of Sound Health

There is a fountain of youth: it is your mind, your talents, the creativity you bring to your life and the lives of people you love. When you learn to tap this source, you will truly have defeated age.

— *Sophia Loren*

Go to bed praying and get up singing and notice what a fine day's work you will do.
— *Napoleon Hill*

Day 282

Maintenance of Sound Health

The biggest disease this day and age is that of people feeling unloved.

— Princess Diana

Mental germs not only poison the psychological system, but attack a person's physical system as well.

— Napoleon Hill

Day 283

October 11

Maintenance of Sound Health

Raising your awareness of the relationship between food and health is always a good starting point for improving the quality of your life.

— Barbara Berger

Eat right, think right, sleep right, and play right, and you can save the doctor's bill for your vacation money.

— Napoleon Hill

Day 284

Maintenance of Sound Health

*The cure for anything is salt water —
sweat, tears, or the sea.*

— Isak Dinesen

*Don't try to cure a headache. It's better to
cure the thing that caused it.*

— Napoleon Hill

Day 285

October 13

Maintenance of Sound Health

Guidance and support are there for those who have the eyes to see, the ears to hear, and the heart to accept what the Universe has to offer.

— Sonia Choquette

As we are one with the world about us, so are we one with ourselves: a mind-body. And as we are affected by the world we live in, and in turn affect that world, so our body influences our mind, and in turn our mind influences our body.

— Napoleon Hill

Day 286

Maintenance of Sound Health

Women need real moments of solitude and self-reflection to balance out how much of ourselves we give away.

— *Barbara De Angelis*

The most successful person uses autosuggestion as a medium for feeding her mind with the thoughts of things and circumstances she desires, including a health consciousness.

— *Napoleon Hill*

Day 287

October 15
Maintenance of Sound Health

Never go to a doctor whose office plants have died.

> *— Erma Bombeck*

Some live to eat, others eat to live, and they live better and longer.

> *— Napoleon Hill*

Day 288

Budgeting Time and Money

People are divided into two classes: drifters and non-drifters. A non-drifter is a person who has a definite major purpose, a definite plan to attain that purpose, and is busily engaged in carrying out his plan. A drifter does no real thinking. He acts upon the thinking of others.

Successful people ask themselves the following questions:

· How are you using your time?

· How much of it are you wasting, and

· How are you wasting it?

· What are you doing to stop this waste?

· Tell me how you use your spare time and how you spend your money, and I will tell you where and what you will be ten years from now.

It is easy to say 'no' when you understand what you desire.

— Phyllis Baker

October 16
Budgeting Time and Money

We say we waste time, but that is impossible. We waste ourselves.

— Alice Bloch

Yesterday is gone forever, now make the most of today and tomorrow if you wish to make up for lost time.

— Napoleon Hill

Day 289

Budgeting Time and Money

Imagine waking up every morning and discovering a list of all the things that make you great. Well, don't just imagine it . . . do it!

— *Nancy E. Krulik*

Every woman needs to stop, look, listen and think. And she should do this with regularity, with purpose aforethought. She should take personal inventory of herself at least once a month, to make sure that she is getting the most out of life, or to find out why she is not.

— *Napoleon Hill*

Day 290

October 18
Budgeting Time and Money

I've been on a calendar, but never on time.
— Marilyn Monroe

Remember also that you will never be ready to receive the better things of life which you desire unless you put yourself under a strict system of self-discipline in the use of your time.

— Napoleon Hill

Day 291

Budgeting Time and Money

*Change your mind about money today
and change your experience with money
tomorrow. Try it and see.*

— Chellie Campbell

*Every woman is where she is, and what
she is, because of the habits she has
acquired. The woman who lives up to the
limit of her income, or beyond it, never is a
free woman.*

— Napoleon Hill

Day 292

October 20

Budgeting Time and Money

Just about the time you think you can make both ends meet, somebody moves the ends.

— *Pansy Penner*

Frugality is one of the essentials of success. The habit of planned savings encourages frugality, makes it an established habit.

— *Napoleon Hill*

Day 293

Budgeting Time and Money

When I'm about to take a risk, I consider the down side. If it's not death, I do it.

— *Nancy Sardella*

Self-examination requires self-discipline, courage, sincerity and a willingness to face facts. Successful women always are their own most severe critics and taskmasters. They maneuver the circumstances of their lives to their own advantage, instead of procrastinating and allowing circumstances to maneuver them into failure.

— *Napoleon Hill*

Day 294

Budgeting Time and Money

What you love is as unique to you as your fingerprints. You need to know that because nothing will make you really happy but doing what you love.

— Barbara Sher

The happiest women are those who have learned to mix play with their work and bind the two together with enthusiasm.

— Napoleon Hill

Budgeting Time and Money

*I've been rich and I've been poor. Rich is
better.*

— *Sophie Tucker*

*The major purpose of a budget system is to
establish habits which force one to save a
definite percentage of her income so that
eventually she may acquire economic
independence.*

— *Napoleon Hill*

Day 296

October 24

Budgeting Time and Money

If you want more, pay more.

— Stella Adler

*Readiness calls for preparation through
the conditioning of your mind to accept
guidance from within.*

— Napoleon Hill

Day 297

Budgeting Time and Money

*Self-respect is a question of recognizing
that anything worth having has its price.*
— *Joan Didion*

*The Creator gave you a brain to be used
and constant access to the power of
thought which flows into your brain from
the great storehouse of Infinite
Intelligence. What use are you making of
this power?*
— *Napoleon Hill*

Day 298

October 26

Budgeting Time and Money

Money is like manure—it's not worth anything unless you spread it around.

— Dolly Levi

Use your time wisely. Invest it in creating relationships which are mutually rewarding and harmonious.

— Napoleon Hill

Day 299

Budgeting Time and Money

Yesterday is a canceled check, tomorrow is a promissory note, today is ready cash — use it.

— *Kay Lyons*

If you wish a job done promptly and well, get a busy woman to do it.

— *Napoleon Hill*

Day 300

Budgeting Time and Money

All shall be well
and all shall be well
and all manner of thing shall be well.
— *Julian of Norwich*

Clear your mind of all anxieties, all
desires, all fears, and give your Creator an
opportunity to speak to you.
— *Napoleon Hill*

Day 301

Budgeting Time and Money

There is no pleasure in having nothing to do; the fun is in having lots to do and not doing it.

— Mary Wilson Little

Yes, your real boss is the person who walks around under your hat. Recognize this truth and you will have an adequate incentive to use your time effectively.

— Napoleon Hill

Day 302

October 30

Budgeting Time and Money

It is the simple things of life that make living worthwhile, the sweet fundamental things such as love and duty, work and rest, and living close to nature.

— *Laura Ingalls Wilder*

By freeing your mind for one hour each day you will be inviting opportunity to reveal itself to you.

— *Napoleon Hill*

Day 303

Budgeting Time and Money

A woman's best protection is a little money of her own.

— Clare Booth Luce

Make your money work for you and you will not have to work so hard for it.

— Napoleon Hill

Day 304

Creative Vision

Creative Vision is developed by the free and fearless use of one's imagination. Creative Vision attains its ends by basically new ideas and methods. It is not a miraculous quality with which one is gifted or is not gifted at birth. It is a quality that may be developed. It may be an inborn quality of mind, or an acquired quality, for it may be developed by the free and fearless use of the faculty of imagination. Our country needs Creative Vision now as it has never needed it before.

By imagining something first, I was able to actually make the vision become a reality.
— Thelzeda Moore

November 1
Creative Vision

The next time your mind wanders, follow it around for awhile.

> — *Jessica Masterson*

Creative Vision is the capacity to envision new possibilities, dream new dreams, and tap into the vast powers of the universe which permit you to build a new tomorrow as you achieve your Definite Major Purpose.

> — *Napoleon Hill*

Day 305

Creative Vision

When you obey all the rules, you miss all the fun.

— Katherine Hepburn

Creative Vision is much more than simply a game of "let's try and think of a new idea."

— Napoleon Hill

Day 306

November 3

Creative Vision

Memory feeds imagination.

— Amy Tan

*A woman introspects, which means she is
capable of "tuning" in to her inner self.*

— Napoleon Hill

Day 307

Creative Vision

Before you can do something that you've never done before, you have to be able to imagine it's possible.

— Jean Shinoda Bolen

Imagination is the key to all achievement, the mainspring of all human endeavor, and the secret door leading to the inner-woman.

— Napoleon Hill

Day 308

November 5

Creative Vision

It is the creative potential itself in human beings that is the image of God.

— Mary Daly

Creative Vision is more tuned to the creative spirit of the universe which expresses itself through woman.

— Napoleon Hill

Day 309

Creative Vision

Imagination is the highest kite one can fly.

— Lauren Bacall

Creative Vision is reserved for the sensitive, inspired, open-ended person who enjoys life and wishes to drink from its deepest wells.

— Napoleon Hill

Day 310

November 7

Creative Vision

Today is the full bloom of life. The petals of yesterday have shriveled in the past. Tomorrow is an unopened bud that may be blackened by the frost or beautified by the sun of life.

— *Coletta Davidson*

Imagination is the soil within which flowers the creative effort distinguishing winners from losers.

— *Napoleon Hill*

Day 311

Creative Vision

Each one of us is God's special work of art.
Through us, He teaches and inspires . . .
those who view our lives.

— Joni Eareckson Tada

Creative Vision is definitely related to that
state of mind known as Faith, and it is
deeply significant that those who have
demonstrated the greatest amount of
creative vision are known to have been
women with a great capacity for faith.

— Napoleon Hill

Day 312

November 9

Creative Vision

Every thought we think is creating our future.

— Louise L. Hay

Creative Vision is not a miraculous quality with which one is gifted or not gifted at birth.

— Napoleon Hill

Day 313

Creative Vision

Sometimes the only way to tell if there's an open door is to try to step through it.

— Heidi S. Hess

Creative Vision is a quality which may be developed.

— Napoleon Hill

November 11
Creative Vision

Defining myself, as opposed to being defined by others, is one of the most difficult challenges I face.
— *Carol Moseley-Braun*

Creative Vision assists you in discovering who you are, what you want from life, and what you are willing to give in return.
— *Napoleon Hill*

Day 315

Creative Vision

Creativity is . . . seeing something that doesn't exist already. You need to find out how you can bring it into being and that way be a playmate with God.

—Michele Shea

The dare to do spirit of Creative Vision inspires women to pioneer and experiment in every field of endeavor.

— Napoleon Hill

Day 316

November 13
Creative Vision

The most lethal weapon in the world's arsenal is not the neutron bomb or chemical warfare but the human mind that devises such things and puts them to use.

— *Margaret Atwood*

Our country needs Creative Vision now as it has never needed it before.

— *Napoleon Hill*

Day 317

Creative Vision

*The world is wide, and I will not waste
my life in friction when it could be turned
into momentum.*

— *Frances Willard*

*Our nation has plenty of brawn and
muscle – but what is needed desperately is
an outpouring of Creative Vision if we are
to meet the very complex demands we now
face and surmount the crisis of complex
international relationships upon which
the peace and prosperity of the world
depends.*

— *Napoleon Hill*

Day 318

November 15

Creative Vision

For each of us as women, there is a deep place within, where hidden and growing our true spirit rises. . . . Within these deep places, each one holds an incredible reserve of creativity and power, of unexamined and unrecorded emotion and feeling.

— *Audre Lorde*

Adopt the habit of the "silent hour" when you will be still and listen for that small, still voice that speaks from within, thus discovering the greatest of all power, Creative Vision, the great power that can help you achieve your Definite Major Purpose.

— *Napoleon Hill*

Day 319

Creative Vision

Woman, if the soul of the nation is to be saved, I believe that you must become its soul.

— Coretta Scott King

The woman possessing Creative Vision knows that she succeeds only by helping others to succeed, and she knows that it is not necessary for another woman to fail in order that she may succeed.

— Napoleon Hill

Day 320

November 17
Creative Vision

To gain what is worth having, it may be necessary to lose everything else.

— *Bernadette Devlin*

A woman with Creative Vision knows what she desires of life and understands that life never permits anyone to get something of value for nothing without eventually having to pay more for it than it is worth.

— *Napoleon Hill*

Day 321

Creative Vision

Believe in something larger than yourself.
. . . Get involved in some of the big ideas
of your time.

— *Barbara Bush*

Creative Vision is a quality of mind
belonging only to women who follow the
habit of Going the Extra Mile. It
recognizes no such thing as the regularity
of working hours and it is not primarily
concerned with monetary compensation as
its highest aim is to achieve the
"impossible."

— *Napoleon Hill*

Day 322

November 19

Creative Vision

I think the key is for women not to set any limits.

— Martina Navratilova

The woman with Creative Vision knows where she is going.

— Napoleon Hill

Day 323

Creative Vision

We would like to believe that we are not in the business of surviving but in being good, and we do not like to admit to ourselves that we are good in order to survive.

— Dorothy Rowe

The woman with Creative Vision has no fear of others, either those of higher or lower rank, for she is at peace with herself and is fair and honest in her relationships with others and herself.

— Napoleon Hill

Day 324

November 21

Creative Vision

I soon realized that no journey carries one far unless, as it extends into the world around us, it goes an equal distance into the world within.

— Lillian Smith

You must go into the silence alone of your own free will and accord.

— Napoleon Hill

Day 325

Creative Vision

Energy creates energy. It is by spending oneself that one becomes rich.

— Sarah Bernhardt

The woman with Creative Vision produces results, not excuses.

— Napoleon Hill

Day 326

November 23
Creative Vision

Don't be afraid of the space between your dreams and reality. If you can dream it, you can make it so.

— *Belva Davis*

Developing Creative Vision keeps a woman so busy achieving her Definite Major Purpose that there is not time left for worry and doubt or fear and frustration.

— *Napoleon Hill*

Day 327

Creative Vision

I realized that if what we call human nature can be changed, then absolutely anything is possible. And from that moment, my life changed.

— Shirley MacLaine

It is a well-known fact that any idea, plan or purpose, that is brought into the conscious mind repeatedly and supported by the emotional feeling is automatically picked up by the subconscious section of the mind and carried out to its logical conclusion by means of whatever practical media are at hand.

— Napoleon Hill

Day 328

November 25

Creative Vision

As we become purer channels for God's light, we develop an appetite for the sweetness that is possible in this world. A miracle worker is not geared toward fighting the world that is, but toward creating the world that could be.
—Marianne Williamson

The imagination has been described as "the workshop of the soul wherein is shaped all plans for individual achievement."
— Napoleon Hill

Day 329

Creative Vision

*But this freedom is only the beginning; the
room is your own, but it is still bare. It
has to be furnished; it has to be decorated;
it has to be shared. How are you going to
furnish it, how are you going to decorate
it? With whom are you going to share it,
and upon what terms?*

— Virginia Woolf

*Locked deep within the human spirit is a
vast reservoir of ideas and insights
waiting to be released.*

— Napoleon Hill

Day 330

November 27

Creative Vision

*The cure for boredom is curiosity. There
is no cure for curiosity.*

— *Ellen Parr*

*Nearly every fact or idea known to man is
but a combination of older realities
rearranged to create a new appearance
or synthesis. This is synthetic
imagination.*

— *Napoleon Hill*

Day 331

Creative Vision

The only thing that makes life possible is permanent, intolerable uncertainty; not knowing what comes next.

— Ursula K. LeGuin

The other type of imagination is Creative Imagination which has its base in the subconscious section of the mind and serves as the medium by which new facts or ideas are revealed through the faculty known as the "sixth sense."

— Napoleon Hill

Day 332

November 29

Creative Vision

"But it is always interesting when one doesn't see," she added. "If you don't see what a thing means, you must be looking at it wrong way around."

— *Agatha Christie*

The soil within which great creative efforts blossom can be enriched by applying the seventeen success principles; i.e., the Science of Success.

— *Napoleon Hill*

Day 333

Creative Vision

*People are like stained glass windows—
the true beauty can be seen only when
there is light from within. The darker the
night, the brighter the windows.*
> *— Elisabeth Kübler-Ross*

*The point can be made – "It makes little
difference where a woman begins."*
> *— Napoleon Hill*

Day 334

Cosmic Habitforce

Cosmic Habitforce pertains to the universe as a whole and the laws that govern it. Cosmic Habitforce is Infinite Intelligence in operation. It is a sense of order. It takes over a habit and causes a person to act upon the habit automatically. Developing and establishing positive habits leads to peace of mind, health, and financial security. You are where you are and what you are because of your established habits and thoughts and deeds.

I tell others that first you get a good habit and then it will carry you to wherever you want to go.

— Yang Ping

December 1

Cosmic Habitforce

Where thou art, that is Home.
— Emily Dickinson

The orderliness of the world gives evidence that all natural laws are under the control of a universal plan.
— Napoleon Hill

Day 335

Cosmic Habitforce

Hurt No Living Thing
Hurt no living thing;
Ladybird, nor butterfly,
Nor moth with dusty wing,
Nor cricket chirping cheerily,
Nor grasshopper so light of leap,
Nor dancing gnat, not beetle fat,
Nor harmless worms that creep.
— *Christina Rossetti*

Cosmic Habitforce pertains to the entire
universe and is the law by which the
equilibrium of the universe is maintained
through established patterns or habits.
— *Napoleon Hill*

Day 336

December 3

Cosmic Habitforce

I share Einstein's affirmation that anyone who is not lost on the rapturous awe at the power and glory of the mind behind the universe "is as good as a burnt out candle."

— *Madeleine L'Engle*

Cosmic Habitforce is Infinite Intelligence in action.

— *Napoleon Hill*

Day 337

Cosmic Habitforce

Here's the good news: God is a nag. God won't give up. If we are destined to carry out some divine idea, we won't be able to shrug it off. For me, God doesn't just whisper within. If I'm supposed to get a message, I start to see it and hear it everywhere—books, sermons, television shows, conversations with friends.
— *Ellen Debenport*

Be sure to make your plan sufficiently flexible so that you can change it any time that you are inspired to do so . . . Infinite Intelligence may hand you a better plan than the one you have made for yourself for the achievement of your purpose.
— *Napoleon Hill*

Day 338

December 5
Cosmic Habitforce

We all have the extraordinary coded within us waiting to be released.

— Jean Houston

Nothing is ever produced which does not bear many, or all, of the characteristics of its ancestors.

— Napoleon Hill

Day 339

Cosmic Habitforce

The horizon leans forward, offering you space to place new steps of change.

— Maya Angelou

If you treat hunches as foolish ideas, they will soon treat you the same way and stay away. When you have a hunch, no matter how foolish it may seem, put it down on paper. Examine it carefully, and you may find that it may be an assist from Infinite Intelligence intended to put you back on the beam, when you may have gotten off.

— Napoleon Hill

Day 340

December 7

Cosmic Habitforce

*Today I know that I cannot control the
ocean tides. I can only go with the flow.*

— Marie Stilkind

*Cosmic Habitforce is the law which forces
every living creature, and every particle of
matter, to come under the dominating
influence of its environment, including the
physical habits and thought habits of
mankind.*

— Napoleon Hill

Day 341

Cosmic Habitforce

Nature does not ask permission. Blossom and birth whenever you feel like it.

— *Clarissa Pinkola Estes*

Control your mental attitude, keep it positive by exercising self-discipline, and thus prepare the mental soil in which any worthwhile plan, purpose or desire may be planted by repeated, intense impression, with the assurance that it will germinate, grow and find expression ultimately in its material equivalent, through whatever means are at hand.

— *Napoleon Hill*

Day 342

December 9
Cosmic Habitforce

Whether we are poets or parents or teachers or artists or gardeners, we must start where we are and use what we have. . . . What seems mundane and trivial may show itself to be holy, precious, part of a pattern.

— *Luci Shaw*

Nature and the universe are organized and ordered. This order, or reliability, of nature simplifies life.

— *Napoleon Hill*

Day 343

Cosmic Habitforce

Originality is not doing something no one else has ever done, but doing what has been done countless times with new life, new breath.

— *Marie Chapian*

Time, space, energy, matter and intelligence are nature's building blocks with which she creates all things.

— *Napoleon Hill*

Day 344

December 11
Cosmic Habitforce

*In the end, what affects your life most
deeply are things too simple to talk about.*
— Nell Blaine

*An oak tree grows from an acorn, and a
pine tree grows from a pine nut. An acorn
never produces a pine tree, nor does a pine
nut produce an oak tree. Nothing is ever
produced which does not bear many, or
all, of the characteristics of its ancestors.*
— Napoleon Hill

Day 345

Cosmic Habitforce

Success doesn't come to you, you go get it.
— *Marva Collins*

*There is nothing that is not controlled by
this universal law of Cosmic Habitforce.*
— *Napoleon Hill*

Day 346

December 13

Cosmic Habitforce

*Waiting until everything is perfect before
making a move is like waiting to start a
trip until all the traffic lights are green.*
— *Karen Ireland*

*Negative thought habits attract to their
creator physical manifestations
corresponding to their nature as perfectly
and as inevitably as nature germinates
the acorn and develops it into an oak tree.*
— *Napoleon Hill*

Day 347

Cosmic Habitforce

We need to approach our state of mind with curiosity and open wonder. That curious listening to life is a joy—no matter what the mood of our life is.

—Charlotte Joko Beck

As we have seen, our thought habits, our mental attitude, are the one and only things over which each individual has the right of complete control.

— Napoleon Hill

Day 348

December 15

Cosmic Habitforce

There is only one path to Heaven. On Earth, we call it Love.

— Karen Goldman

All voluntary positive habits are the products of will power directed toward the attainment of definite goals.

— Napoleon Hill

Day 349

Cosmic Habitforce

Remember that you are all people and that all people are you. Remember that you are this universe and that this universe is you.

— Joy Harjo

Women are all born equal in the sense that they have equal access to this great principle. All normal persons have the right to control their thoughts and their mental attitude, and this is the way in which this greatest of all natural laws is made effective in individual lives.

— Napoleon Hill

Day 350

December 17
Cosmic Habitforce

We stand now where two roads diverge. But unlike the roads in Robert Frost's familiar poem, they are not equally fair. The road we have long been traveling is deceptively easy, a smooth superhighway on which we progress with great speed, but at its end lies disaster. The other fork of the road—the "one less traveled by"—offers our last, our only chance to reach a destination that assures the preservation of the earth.

— *Rachel Carson*

All big things are composed of smaller things of a related nature.

— *Napoleon Hill*

Day 351

Cosmic Habitforce

*Never, never rest contented with any circle
of ideas, but always be certain that a
wider one is still possible.*

— Pearl Bailey

*Cosmic Habitforce has the capacity to
impart a peculiar quality to one's habits of
thought which removes obstacles and
provides a power capable of surmounting
barriers to success.*

— Napoleon Hill

Day 352

December 19

Cosmic Habitforce

Learn to practice.

— Martha Graham

Our habits are created through repeated thought and experience.

— Napoleon Hill

Day 353

Cosmic Habitforce

Desire, ask, believe, receive.
> — *Stella Terrill Mann*

Cosmic Habitforce is the comptroller of all natural laws.
> — *Napoleon Hill*

Day 354

December 21
Cosmic Habitforce

For visions come not to polluted eyes.
> *— Mary Howitt*

It's a great moment in your life when you break away from your social heredity and start doing your own thinking.
> *— Napoleon Hill*

Day 355

Cosmic Habitforce

*The dream is real, my friends. The failure
to realize it is the only unreality.*

— Toni Cade Bambara

*If you allow the fear of criticism, doubt
and other people's negative suggestions to
take shape in your mind, it will blot out
the picture of your major purpose.*

— Napoleon Hill

Day 356

December 23
Cosmic Habitforce

*We have been taught to believe that
negative equals realistic and positive
equals unrealistic.*

— Susan Jeffers

*The same law which holds our earth in its
orbit and relates it to all other planets in
their orbits, both in time and space,
relates human beings to one another in
exact conformity with the nature of their
own thoughts.*

— Napoleon Hill

Day 357

Cosmic Habitforce

I've arrived at this outermost edge of my life by my own actions. Where I am is thoroughly unacceptable. Therefore, I must stop doing what I've been doing.

— Alice Killer

When you speak of your ambitions, if at all, use the past tense, after they have become accomplishments and are not just words.

— Napoleon Hill

Day 358

December 25
Cosmic Habitforce

Whether you know it or not, fear has developed your likes and dislikes, picked your friends, and raised your children.

— *Rhonda Britten*

Mental habits as well, including both poverty consciousness and prosperity consciousness, are fixed through the law of Cosmic Habitforce.

— *Napoleon Hill*

Day 359

Cosmic Habitforce

I have a simple philosophy. Fill what's empty. Empty what's full. And scratch where it itches.

— Alice Roosevelt Longworth

The stars and planets operate with clocklike precision. They never collide, never get off their appointed course, but roll on eternally, as the result of a preconceived plan.

— Napoleon Hill

Day 360

December 27

Cosmic Habitforce

To be able to be caught up into the world of thought -- that is being educated.

— Edith Hamilton

Let us repeat once more, for the sake of emphasis: your mind acts like an electro-magnet to attract to you the things upon which you keep it focused.

— Napoleon Hill

Day 361

Cosmic Habitforce

There never was night that had no morn.
— Dinah Mulock Craik

The major distinguishing characteristic of Cosmic Habitforce is that it forces all repeated actions to become fixed habits, whether these be the thoughts of a person or the orderly movement of the stars or the coming and going of the seasons.
— Napoleon Hill

Day 362

December 29
Cosmic Habitforce

Some tension is necessary for the soul to grow, and we can put that tension to good use. We can look for every opportunity to give and receive love, to appreciate nature, to heal our wounds and the wounds of others, to forgive and to serve.

— *Joan Borysenko*

A strong will does not dwell on the past. A vital ego thrives on the hopes and desires of the yet unattained objective.

— *Napoleon Hill*

Day 363

Cosmic Habitforce

*The game of life is a game of boomerangs.
Our thoughts, deeds and words return to
us sooner or later with astounding
accuracy.*

— Florence Scovel Shinn

*You are where you are and what you are
because of your established habits of
thoughts and deeds.*

— Napoleon Hill

Day 364

December 31
Cosmic Habitforce

Put your ear down close to your soul and listen hard.

— Anne Sexton

You now understand why the greatest of all riches is a Positive Mental Attitude, for by means of such an attitude it is possible to acquire all other things which you may rightfully desire and possess.

What the mind can conceive and believe, it can achieve with PMA!

— Napoleon Hill

Day 365

Made in the USA
Middletown, DE
24 September 2023

39238354R00236